The Sphere of Art
And the Two Sensitive Points
by
R. J. Stewart

Includes the original Inner Temple Traditions
Inner Convocation™ meditations

and teachings developed from
conversations with A. R. Heaver "Zadok" (1900-1980)

R. J. Stewart Books

The Sphere of Art
By R. J. Stewart

Published by:
R. J. Stewart Books

First Edition
Printed in the United States of America

A Catalogue record for this book is available from the Library of Congress.

ISBN: 978-0-9791402-6-6

An Inner Temple Traditions InnerConvocation™ ® Publication

R. J. Stewart Books
P.O. Box 802
Arcata, CA 95518
www.rjstewart.net

Biography

R.J. Stewart is a Scottish author, musician and composer of international acclaim, who has composed for theater, film, and television, toured as a concert performer, and has made many recordings of his own music. He lives in a remote part of northern California.

R. J. Stewart has worked, researched and written extensively on the spiritual and magical core of the Western esoteric traditions, with 40 books in publication translated into many languages worldwide. He works with myth, imagination, music, and the primal magical arts of inner transformation and vision.

Since 1988 he has concentrated mainly on writing, and teaching small groups in Europe and the USA, specifically working towards regenerating ancient traditions of inner transformation for practical modern use.

The Sphere of Art is the most advanced set of techniques within The Inner Temple Traditions/Inner Convocation program taught internationally by R. J. Stewart from 1988 to the present day.

Acknowledgements

I wish to acknowledge the profound influence of Alfred Ronald Heaver (1900-1980), the work of W. G. Gray, Kathleen Raine, and the continuing support of Gareth Knight. Also the many students and friends who have worked with me in opening the Sphere of Art for the 21st century.

Selected Titles
by R. J. Stewart
for Inner Temple Traditions Inner Convocation work

Living Magical Arts
1986 UK and subsequent USA editions

Advanced Magical Arts
1988 UK and subsequent USA editions

The Spiritual Dimension of Music
1987 UK and subsequent USA editions

Music Power Harmony
1988/2008

The Miracle Tree
2003 USA

The UnderWorld Initiation
1985 UK and subsequent USA editions

See www.rjstewart.net
for a full list of books and recordings.

Table of Contents

Foreword

This is an important book that you hold in your hands. Do not be misled by its real or apparent simplicity. Whatever you paid for it – or if it came into your hands by any other means – you may rest assured that it is a pearl of great price.

Its genesis is the result of a veritable distillation of knowledge and experience that has been imparted by personal contact through a series of practitioners down the generations. Each one of whom has had the good fortune and wit – or even predestination – to be able to identify, on the one hand a valid teacher, and the other a worthwhile student. Thus has the torch of inspiration been passed along to your present benefit. To receive it, all you have to do is work with it sincerely.

R J Stewart has been personally known to me for many years and although our paths have been different, sometimes as of water to fire, in the light of experience they appear to have been as complementary as the serpents that ascend the staff of the caduceus of Hermes. I therefore heartily commend this book to you as being well worth your applied attention and best intentions. The rest is up to you.

— *Gareth Knight*

Preface to Volume One:
The Sphere of Art

For some years I have been listening to people give talks on spiritual subjects, mainly at conferences or events where I am giving a concert or speaking myself. I have heard many wonderful and inspiring things, and I am grateful to live in a time and in a culture where such things are allowed. Nevertheless, I must admit to a deep dissatisfaction with one trend that seems widespread: speakers, often highly acclaimed authors and teachers, repeatedly talk only about their own experiences. "When in Prague I had a vision of X" or "That night I sensed a spirit enter the room" or "The Masters gave me this message…". If you have attended any such events, you will have heard many talks of this sort. What I want to hear is *how can we have such experiences for ourselves?* (with the exception of messages from the Masters, who always seem so vague and out of touch). How can we have such experiences for ourselves? We need not to merely hear stories about spiritual perception, but to come into spiritual perception for ourselves. My aim for some years has been to offer techniques and explorations that do just that, whereby the student can have actual experience and not be restricted to hearing or reading about what happened to someone else, no matter how remarkable it may be.

The Sphere of Art and the Two Sensitive Points took more than 30 years to develop in the present form, yet the practices, once they are grasped, are simple and brief. Before writing this book, I spent some time teaching the material to small groups of advanced students in several locations in the USA, and opened out the broader aspects at larger gatherings in Britain, (between 2004 and 2008 in Glastonbury Town Hall and at Hawkwood College, Stroud, both key locations in Britain for the seeding of new spiritual impetus). In group work we found that a verbal teaching could be grasped quickly; the problem with text on magical arts is that the reader really has to *do it* before some aspects of the text become clear. Of course, we should understand this as a process of elucidation through experience, and therefore not a problem at all.

I am aware that many readers "dip into" books on magical arts, rather than study them in full. That will not work with these books. They are intentionally short and concentrated. You have to steadily read them through from the beginning to the end, chapter by chapter before attempting the forms and practices described. Indeed, I always recommend that all esoteric books be read through as a complete story, before attempting any exercises. By doing this, you will have already attuned your mind to the subject matter before deeper practice, rather than flit through fragments of it in a state of mildly curious distraction similar to channel surfing on television.

The text is in two volumes: the first, *The Sphere of Art,* is a short condensed exploration and exposition with the essential practical forms and basics described. The second, *The Purifying Fire,* explores themes that can only be fully addressed after experiencing the forms and practices described in volume 1.

Both volumes are intended for those who dedicate themselves to focused spiritual work through ethical magical arts. These are not books for beginners, and the techniques and concepts found here are not easy, popularized, or made fashionable. Nor, I hasten to add, are they intentionally obscure: the time for prolix unapproachable texts on alchemy and magic is long since over. When we study texts from earlier centuries, there are many communicative linguistic conceptual and cultural tangles to unravel (to say nothing of errors, misprints, and bad translations): it is unfortunate that this entanglement, which exists for the modern mind through retrospect, has been taken up as "style" by many later writers.

Excessive Capitalization Of Text, a Common Feature in Books on Magical Arts, has been avoided as much as possible, though some is necessary in context.

The aim throughout this book has been to make subjects that are by nature recondite and subtle draw close to the reader, speak with plain language and propose workable practical examples. Most of all, the aim is to bring the student into the practices of the Sphere of Art and the Two Sensitive Points that transform the spiritual life, and thus the outer life. By undertaking this task in ourselves, we begin to transform the world, bringing it into a new condition and redeeming the old. No lesser task is worthy of our magic.

Here is some brief preliminary scouting through the text, whereby the reader may have a simple map of the territory before exploring further.

Volume 1 contains the following categories (not always in the order listed, though mainly organized by chapter):

Category 1: *background, sources, and perennial spiritual traditions relating to the subject matter.*

Category 2: *brief autobiographical context in the development of The Sphere of Art in my writing, teaching, and spiritual life.*

Category 3: *brief biographical context for A R Heaver, the Glastonbury adept known as "Zadok".*

The contents of 1, 2 and 3 above are found mainly in the Introduction, which should be read carefully before the chapters, as it gives substantial context to everything that follows, and describes key concepts and traditions that are essential for understanding the subsequent practical work. There is further discussion under Category 1 in the remaining chapters.

Category 4: *Discussion of forms, methods, and implications of The Sphere of Art and the Two Sensitive Points.*

A number of themes for meditation are included in Category 4, mainly found in Chapters One to Three and both exposition and meditative concepts should be explored and experienced before moving into the techniques and sacromagical forms found in Category 5. This preparation phase is essential, as understanding the exposition and meditating on the concepts suggested, prepares us for the sacromagical forms of the Sphere of Art. After we have learned and practiced the forms, the same meditations will open out further into new dimensions of consciousness, as there is an ongoing interaction between the simple meditative themes (that can be done under most circumstances) and the sacromagical work that can only be done in the finely attuned field of spiritual energy of the Sphere.

Category 5: *Detailed methods of working, stage by stage: these are found in Chapters One to Three, typically but not exclusively at the end of each chapter.*

Category 6: *Appendices and Bibliography, support material and further reading/research.*

The contents of Categories 4 and 5 are found in the Chapters One to Three and Category 6 above includes articles, exercises, and previously published foundational techniques, as additional support material.

Content of Volume 2: The Purifying Fire

Brief references are made throughout to Volume 2, citing themes that will be developed at length. Volume 2 focuses on three main themes:

1 The relationship between the Arimathean and Arthurian traditions in practical sacromagical work, though not in a mythic historical or literary sense (as there are many books that do so already).

2 The alchemical text *Aesch Mezareph:* again from a practical perspective in spiritual magic, not as historic literature or psychological reductionism.

3 The relationship between sacromagical mediation (the art of the magician priestess and priest) and prophecy.

If you take up this work, you will be joining a contemporary community that continues an ongoing sacromagical task that began its current phase in the Glastonbury area in the 1950's, as described in our Introduction. This contemporary community comprises a small network of people widely located, in the USA, Canada, Britain, Europe, Egypt, and Brazil. Not a rigid organization, but a living organism of intention, of sacromagical dedication, of consciousness. The "beginning" of this organism in Britain in the 1950's is really an insertion point in time, and, like all such communities regardless of cultural origin, our spiritual impetus has a much longer cycle than that of human generations. Such insertion points may be traced to various centuries, individuals, tasks, and teachings. The true community exists in a consciousness beyond time, a trans-lunar awareness. You can join this greater community through the Sphere of Art.

R. J. Stewart, California, 2008

Introduction

The Sphere of Art is a sacromagical "system". This means, simply, that if you follow the methods described, there will be changes of subtle energy and consciousness that far exceed those changes that are commonly experienced in day to day life, extending beyond personality and individuality into the greater cosmos. Magic is, in itself, a neutral artistic science, which can be used in many ways, good bad or indifferent according to the intention of the user: in our present context there is an ethical quality and stance. The word *sacromagical* is used throughout to mean non-religious/sectarian magical arts, ceremony ritual and related forms, in service of the sacred, and directed towards spiritual evolution. (You may find the word used in varying ways in other sources, especially with an emphasis upon pre-Christian ritual, which we do not mean here. Hence our definition at the outset).

The word *system* is used with caution here, and must be qualified before we go further. No magical system should ever be described as complete: all magical systems are works-in-progress, as they must evolve and transform through interaction. If anything is a complete system, it is already dead, and can only collapse; this law holds good in the higher dimensions just as it does in nature. Once a species has peaked in its expansion, it does not take over and forever dominate its environment, but instead diminishes according to the dynamic homeostasis of nature. Humanity take note! Likewise in spiritual forms and traditions, once a structure has grown sufficiently large, it can only collapse. Some, of course, give forth seeds; the tradition of

Seed Bearers is especially pertinent to our theme here, and we will return to this later.

In Time of Death, Change, and False Authority

We live in the death-throws of those rigid dogmatic Book religions that have cruelly dominated human consciousness for at least two millenniums: in their conflict with one another they seem to exert as much destructive power as possible, determined to bring the world down with them. This is not, as it seems on the surface, a geopolitical struggle, but a spiritual death and rebirth for humanity. Formal religions, from the most ancient times to the present, regardless of their origins or traditions, tend towards a systematized rigidity and dogma...the original impulse has become a "system" which becomes an "authority" which becomes politicized and materially focused: but the original impulse has already gone elsewhere. This was as true of the pagan religions as it has become of the Book religions, and we should not succumb to romantic fantasies about the ancestral past.

The original impulse, however, is still found in esoteric or partly hidden traditions, those deep streams that are suppressed but never destroyed, that re-emerge from time to time into broader consciousness. Expositions of esoteric traditions can, in themselves, become rigid and text bound. We see repeated miniature assertions of authority and consequent collapse in organizations that attempt to embody spiritual impulses, such as occult lodges, pagan and wiccan groups, and alternative spiritual organizations of many varieties. This assertiveness and self-proclamation, inevitably coming to a fall, may be regarded as merely human folly, but it masks that deeper law of growth, seeding, dispersal, and collapse, that is found in nature. The seeds are the true result, not the books, rules, or claims to true authority, and not any "complete system".

One of the greatest secrets of powerful magic is that it must never be completed, finalized, or authorized. Like Peter Pan (so aptly named by J M Barry), it will lose its power if it finally grows up and stagnates...but if it remains open to change, the potentials are unlimited. We can observe this in human lives: many people reach a plateau in their forties, and do not change thereafter. Creative, spiritual, artistic, and inwardly active individuals remain open, and continue to grow and change well into their physical old age. So *The Sphere of Art* is an open system, a work in progress, and only the basic parts are described herein, as much of it comes through direct experience and subtle transmission. *If you follow the steps outlined in each chapter, you will come into this new level of experience.*

In esoteric or occult literature we often find simplistic mechanistic undertones, as the attractive idea of the complete system was used in the 19th and early 20th centuries to describe the methodology of particular magical groups or authors, when it was customary to compare spiritual and magical techniques, and related concepts, to rail-networks, simple physics, or electrical circuits. Later it became fashionable to compare magical techniques to psychological theories, and even our most remarkable pioneers of magical arts sought to justify magic thereby: today we increasingly see that this is merely another form of materialist reductionism. Providing we understand that the system described here is alive…an *organism* rather than an *organization* based upon an inert check-list, we can use the word "system" beneficially. This emphasis on organism rather than organization is significant, and we will return to it later.

Basic Functions of the Sphere of Art

The Sphere of Art and the associated *Two Sensitive Points* enable the magician/priestess/priest or whatever term we choose to describe ourselves, to perform several simple interlaced functions. They are simple, but extremely powerful. They do not involve invocation of deities, association with ancestors or faery or land spirits, nor do they involve "making changes through acts of will", that tempting and common fallacy, so often described and copied in popular books, that inflates the ego and substantially disempowers the magician. Most of our action within the Sphere of Art consists of exclusion: all of the above are respectfully and positively excluded, along with many other influences, by the action of the Sphere. There is no concept of negation, rejection, dualism, in any of this, only of specific function.

The simple interlaced functions mentioned above open the Sphere to defined spiritual forces, that have a both a stellar and a telluric resonance, bringing those forces together within a magical ground or energetic field, established inside the Sphere. As we are also inside the Sphere, this interaction has a powerful effect upon us. Sacromagical work within the Sphere embodies an open-ended system that is at once simple, having only minimal components free of text, and yet advanced, reaching far beyond our standard magical methods found in publication and group work at this time.

And, best of all, it works. Read this book, try the methods described, and you will find that it never fails to work. I have been teaching this system or set of magical forms to small groups for several years, and everyone from the most experienced to the relative newcomer to magical arts is astonished at the consistency, clarity, and focus of this material. Not only does it work, but once we have started to participate, it works powerfully every time we engage, and continues to work in the background.

Therefore a word or two of caution. Do not undertake this lightly: it is not a weekend social activity or a fun experiment. Induction into sacromagical power brings responsibility and transformation. If you do not want such responsibility, if you seek escape rather than transformation, do not do this.

Traditional Sources for the Sphere of Art

Multiple interlaced sources may be generally identified in association with The Sphere of Art, including esoteric traditions of alchemy, Hermetic metaphysical philosophy, and what is broadly called Western ritual magic. We may also see general connections, at a basic level, to traditions of spiritual martial arts and spiritual yoga (that is, the forms that are involved in subtle energies and spiritual consciousness rather than circus tricks or gymnastics). All such broad identifications lead into vast oceans of material, often replete with flotsam. What we need, more than ever at this time, are focused clear systems of spiritual magic that deliver: the Sphere of Art is one such. We should think of it as a specialized contemporary refinement of certain techniques that can be traced, often deeply hidden or obscure, through many sources.

It would be more helpful for us, as practitioners, to understand that the specific practices outlined herein will give us deep insights into those traditional sources listed above, rather than cite the sources as authorities *per se*. In all spiritual practices, tradition is vitally important as both a context and a source of drive, ground, and interaction: but it cannot be an "authority", for its very nature as a collective flowing river, rather than a rigid rock, disposes of authority. So in this Introduction, I refer to various traditions in various ways, but no single source or group of sources is offered as a definitive authority, and most of the work in the following pages comprises new developments for the 21st century. The key that unlocks understanding is in an organic process, rather than a state of rigid organization.

Specific Sources and Connections

As *The Sphere of Art* and *The Two Sensitive Points* comprise a unique set of practices in sacromagical arts, I will describe briefly the sources that I drew upon to present this material, and, more significantly, to develop it in my own practices over more than 30 years. They are as follows:

1 The contemporary western magical revolution and re-evaluation as embodied by mentors and explorers of the 20th century. These include, but are not limited to, Dion Fortune, Israel Regardie, W.E. Butler, Gareth Knight, W. G. Gray. In this context, my own publications over the last 30 years, from 1976 onwards, include a steady progression that leads up to The Sphere of Art. This is shown in our Table 1. I hasten to add that I am not asking you to read all or any of these books to practice the Sphere...they represent a development over a number of years, and are offered only to give background and context for this new form.

2 Esoteric alchemy: especially the revival of the art that occurred in France during the early 20th century, and continues quietly to this day, albeit connected to the perennial enduring alchemical traditions. By esoteric alchemy I mean neither the popular idea of the seemingly miraculous transformation of base metals into gold or silver, nor the Jungian concept of alchemy as an internal psychological process, which has generated more obfuscation of alchemy than any other. To the practitioner of the Hermetic esoteric traditions, both of these interpretations of alchemy are simplistic nonsense, serving

only to distract the student into fruitless paths, sometimes for many years. In the case of Jung's approach to alchemy, we find alchemical themes and vocabulary hijacked into a psychological model that seems attractive, even revealing, but on closer analysis is merely self-serving and self-referential. It is nothing more than a closed loop in which alchemical concepts are used as substitutes for psychological concepts, and suddenly, bingo, that confusing old alchemy was, is, and ever will be, a proto-psychology striving towards a modern perspective (such as that of Jung!). Rudolph Steiner warned about the fallacies and usurpations inherent in psychology in the early 20th century, at a time when it had not yet peaked[1].

I referred above to the early 20th century revival of practice of esoteric alchemy, as this is a very specific "lineage" of esoteric teaching, practice, and inner or spiritual contact. It seems likely that it reaches far back into the cultural and historical foundations of western philosophy and metaphysics, but our concern here is with an active stream that can be identified. Its better known exponents are among French and Franco-Russian occultists, Rosicrucians, Martinists, and esotericists (including the composer Eric Satie), and especially the active circles around Egyptologist Renee Schwaller de Lubicz, the originator of the emblematic persona of Fulcanelli, author of *The Mystery of the Cathedrals*[2]. In manifest science, the French-Italian alchemist and physicist Louis or Luigi Rota is significant, as some aspects of his work relate to what happens in The Sphere of Art[3]. Many more could be mentioned, and this short list is merely a prelude, should you choose to research further.

Rota's work has been recorded in part, and can be explored through various resources. He is significant in our context because of the interest in Rota expressed by my mentor the late A. R. Heaver, to whom much of the deep impetus and subtle inspiration for aspects of my own work must be attributed.

3 Alfred Ronald Heaver, 1900-1980, was one of the Glastonbury adepts of that remarkable generation that surged in the early 20th century, at the same time as esotericists in France were establishing a new movement of spiritual alchemy, and as British occultists were substantially revising the art, after the monumental rigidity

and denseness of the 19th century. Heaver was a master of simplicity, the hardest spiritual discipline of them all.

ARH (as we shall call him) is almost unknown to the public, but was influential in many ways in the spiritual revival in Britain from the early years of the 20th century, up to the mid-1970's, after which he retired into deep contemplation, until his fully conscious natural death on his 80th birthday, in 1980. It is little known that ARH started what has become the Glastonbury Chalice Well trust, so famous today, that was taken over and ultimately developed by Wesley Tudor Pole. Nor is it generally known that ARH wrote early suggestions regarding the now famous Glastonbury Zodiac theory, attributed to Mrs. Maltwood, and that some of his papers on this subject are in the Maltwood archive. We will return to this zodiacal theme shortly, but in a surprising manner.

In the 1950's, ARH opened a dedicated temple of silence known as the Sanctuary of Avalon. This was a small building in an apple orchard, in the garden of his home, equidistant between Glastonbury and Cadbury Camp. At some time or other, many of the people who were involved in the spiritual and magical revival travelled to Somerset to meet ARH, and in the latter stages such pilgrims included founders of what would become labeled as the New Age movement in Britain, though ARH himself had little patience with this label. They included well known figures such as Peter Caddy (founder of Findhorn) and Sir George Trevelyan, (founder of the Wrekin Trust). A number of occultists and spiritually orientated individuals visited the Sanctuary to meditate in silence, and many younger students or seekers, including myself, were drawn there by mysterious "coincidences".

Memories vary: everyone who went to the Sanctuary of Avalon remembers that it was a shrine of silence, kept plain and virtually empty. I remember it as being converted from a small building such as an old dairy, with thick walls, plain white inside, and small windows. There was some zodiacal imagery carved in modest wooden panels in the four directions, and an empty altar in the east. Dorothy Maclean, one of the Findhorn founders, told me recently that the Sanctuary had been built, not converted, and built entirely without metal. David Spangler, the author and philosopher, remembers being told during a visit to ARH with Peter Caddy, that it was built or converted in silence. In 2007 I received an email from a former BBC producer who stated that a large "Excalibur-like" sword hung in the sanctuary during his visit in the late 1970s.

Whatever the methods used, the significance and purpose of the Sanctuary of Avalon was clear: it was a small empty shrine of silence dedicated and attuned to the Fourfold Name of Being. Anyone who sat and meditated therein came into attunement with potent spiritual forces, focused into the sanctuary like a powerful floodlight. And we took something of that power away within us, resonating in our bodies. The Sphere of Art enables us, today, to open to that same power, and to go some stages further into its mediation.

In the early 1990s I took part in a sacred poetry event in London, speaking and reading along with Kathleen Raine and Sir George Trevelyan, and was taken aback to hear Sir George paraphrase, with typical flamboyant emphasis and drama, an esoteric concept that I had first heard from ARH twenty or more years previous. At that moment, I felt the touch of the spiritual power that had flowed through ARH come through Sir George. We enter into this continuum of spiritual power when we work with the Sphere of Art, not something based on names and personality, but something that touches and inspires us regardless of our personal status or opinion.

I have described my meetings with ARH in articles published by the Glastonbury magazine "Avalon" and on my website, www.rjstewart.org. A slightly revised version of the article is included as an appendix to this book. Through necessity some information is duplicated between the earlier article and this Introduction, but here we focus more precisely on the magical and spiritual themes that lead up to the Sphere of Art.

Before going further, I must emphasize that I did not learn the Sphere of Art from ARH. As mentioned shortly, he did not teach methods, but mediated spiritual power and communion wordlessly or during conversation on a wide range of subjects. The methods described here have been developed through my own work, and embody something new. But the inspiration, the subtle guidance along certain paths, certainly came through contact with ARH, and for many years to follow, with the spiritual power that he mediated.

The Sphere, Subtle Fire, and the Lineage of Zadok

With the long-term development of the Sphere of Art, we come into a subtle realm that permeates all of the above sources in one way or other, all broadly within the Hermetic tradition, but especially the connection between the French alchemists, ARH and others. I refer to ancient and enduring spiritual transformative traditions of *subtle fire* that surface from time to time in evolving forms, then disappear into the underworld for a period of regenerative dormancy.

This is why, our group work today is described as issuing from the Fire Temple, coming to us through the *lineage of Zadok*, to which we will return shortly. There is more than one Fire Temple, and through the Sphere of Art we attune to a specific inner temple and spiritual impetus.

The methods described in the following chapters are my own development, which I practice, and which I have been teaching to small groups of advanced students for the last few years. They are not found elsewhere in any coherent form, and this is the first time they have been published openly. Of course, there are other magical patterns that are comparable, for all magical arts describe and interact with the cosmos, so we should expect, even demand, that we find connections between them. Finding connections is only useful at the beginning of our journey, and what is needed is to work consistently with sacromagical arts, rather than to merely read about them and compare them. Synthesis of spiritual methods comes as a new level of awareness within us, not through dexterous intellectual analysis or textual juggling. The key to effective magical work is to find a method that works, stay with it, and develop it. The way of enervation and confusion is to endlessly compare "systems" and try to synthesize them into some fantastical overview. Only when we are deeply versed in one transformative system can we truly relate to all the others...from that Other Place, the center of the Sphere of consciousness and Being, wherein they all originate.

This book, and the volumes to follow, expound the forms and methods of the Sphere and the sensitive point. Through practice, you can do this work, and by continuing to do it, you will effect powerful changes within yourself and (later) in the surrounding environment. This work also holds a subtle component that is only revealed verbally and through spiritual transmission, never put directly into a text. The textual training and exposition brings us to the point where we are able to receive the subtle transmission. This is explored further in our main chapters, and need not be any kind of stumbling block to the student. Instead, we must see that the methods and forms offered will lead us to the transmission, preparing us to receive something that otherwise might never reach us.

The impetus, the seeds, for this work within the Sphere of Art, can be traced in part to ARH and the transformative *prophetic* traditions of the Fire Temple. This impulse stimulated his interest, from the 1930's to the 1950's, in the French alchemical revival, bearing in mind that the revival rested upon an ancient and revered foundation dating back thousands of years. What ARH was primarily concerned with, in the alchemical context, was the opening of subtle regenerative energies within the body of the planet. As this was also a concern of the early 20th century alchemists, ARH researched and promoted their work, especially that of Luis Rota.

I should add that, to the best of my knowledge, ARH was not involved in the French alchemical movement *per se*, though he was involved in efforts to bring alternative energy sources such as those of Luis Rota into British industry. His true interest was in the deeper planetary change that caused this renascent alchemical and spiritual movement to flourish through a generation of profound exponents. In other words, something of large significance happened at the beginning of the 20th century, and ARH and many others mediated this into manifestation. We in turn benefit from their work, and our task now must be to take it further, for the 21st century and onward.

This deep planetary aspect of the spiritual life and its responsibility, passed on to me along with other seeds through ARH, has permeated my own work both in print teaching and in private, from the early 1970's to the present day. In addition to the UnderWorld telluric fire connection, there is a specific sacromagical prophetic and priestly lineage that carries a spiritual power through time seeking to resonate out to many: this has been all-embracing in my own work, and is epitomized in the Inner Temple Traditions Inner Convocation[4] and Sphere of Art forms.

Other Aspects of Ronald Heaver's Spiritual Work

There were other aspects of Heaver's vigorous and far-reaching spiritual work that have not been of interest to me, and may even seem redundant to the modern reader. Those interests and commitments included a major role in the British Israel movement, from which ARH resigned in his mature years, choosing to follow a more recondite path of spiritual mediation after many years of outer action. Nowadays many people might see the British Israel movement as somewhat cranky and absurd, at best. Certain modern offshoots and movements that claim association, even if they have none in fact, have taken an unhealthy direction, especially those branches of American evangelism and rapturism that make us distinctly uncomfortable and are potentially a threat to world peace, exhibiting the very opposite of everything that ARH and his respected associates worked for. Rapturism and aggressive evangelism, espousing a nuclear Armaggedon with salvation of the few, directly serve the destructive spiritual forces embodied in the nuclear weapons industry...they are a corrupted shadow of the holy light.

While we might shrug off key concepts that were proposed (such as the British being the lost tribes of Israel and so forth), in its heyday British Israel had thousands of members, attracted many profound minds, and even brought an ethical stance to the movers and shakers of British politics. They saw its esoteric philosophy not as a literal matter, but as a highly evocative allegory of spiritual forces at work in world history. To relate to this today, we should refer to the vision of William Blake and the spiritual Jerusalem for its vibrant core, rather than to any subsequent literalist propaganda. When ARH realized, after many years of service, that British Israel was becoming a redundant organization, he resigned, and moved into deeper work. It is that work, and major new developments thereof, since his passing into the spiritual dimensions in 1980, that concern us here.

Transmission of Spiritual Contact and Impetus

I will summarize shortly some of the seeds that ARH planted, that have surfaced repeatedly in my work. I must emphasize that he would not expect to take personal credit for this, as it is part of a continuum of inner consciousness, a lineage of initiation into sac-romagical consciousness and into the responsibilities that come with the acquisition of associated techniques. ARH was not a guru or an occultist. I heard the late W. G. Gray, often bombastic and cynical, but in that moment somewhat in awe and respect, describe ARH as a "senior officer" and "one of the Old Ones". As I have mentioned in my article on my meetings with ARH, he did not "teach" a class in the accepted sense: he did not hold seminars or workshops, and did not publish any books into the mainstream of occult or esoteric pub-lication. What happened in his presence was a spiritual transmission, far greater than any words that were being offered on the surface.

I have aspired towards this transmission in my own spiritual work, and I attune whenever possible to the Inner Contacts who ra-diate this highly focused consciousness and energy. This is the power that informs and permeates my published work. In this lifetime it was first transmitted to me, undeniably brought into my waking consciousness in 1973, by A. R. Heaver, and even at that time, in my early twenties, I was aware that he stood for Many…for a collec-tive of spiritual power, rather than something individual or tempo-ral that could be owned.

ARH opened this spiritual contact out for me in the most off-hand manner, as if it was a conversation that we had long engaged in, and which was merely being renewed: which, of course, was ex-actly the case. He understood this subtlety of the spiritual and inner contact continuum that extends beyond and between incarnations far better than I, and it has taken years for me to finally catch up, wake up, stand up and be counted. These last three phrases will be familiar to British readers who were taught by an older generation… but here I am applying them to service in the spiritual life, not to post-imperialistic ideas of duty.

Zadok and the Order of Justified or Righteous Ones

The manifest forms, methods, and original texts that I have pub-lished are my own creation within time, but the deeper spiritual im-petus is beyond time. Thus while I claim copyright on all my work, as is appropriate and essential in the material world of publishing and media, I do not claim ownership or authority of the hidden tradition itself. ARH went so far as to write his letters and essays under the name of Zadok, which means Priest, rather than use his personal name. If you choose to research the name Zadok, however, you will find many insights and esoteric connections associated with it, both in terms of Qabalah and Biblical mythology or chronicle. The name is associated with the concept of Righteousness and being Justified: in my early book *The UnderWorld Initiation* and in later publications, this idea appears as the influence of a specific line of inner contacts, transhuman beings who seek to work with us in our spiritual evolution. We will explore some of this is in volume 2, but I highly recommend individual research and meditation, beginning with a concordance.

The Zadok tradition itself holds a lineage older than Biblical or Jewish sources, for it is rooted in ancient Persia and the ancestral fire and volcanic temples of both the middle-east and the Mediterranean world. This tradition gave birth to Greek philosophy, especially that of Pythagoras, Empedocles, and Plato. In the esoteric tradition, handed down through the occult lodges, in oral teachings, and in more recent years within a wide variety of texts, an even older source is proposed: we are told that this Fire Temple tradition originated in Atlantis...a theme first described by Plato[5] around 360 BCE, and stated by him to be ancient even in his day: *"...histories tell of a mighty power which unprovoked made an expedition against the whole of Europe and Asia, and to which your city put an end. This power came forth out of the Atlantic Ocean, for in those days the Atlantic was navigable; and there was an island situated in front of the straits which are by you called the Pillars of Heracles; the island was larger than Libya and Asia put together, and was the way to other islands, and from these you might pass to the whole of the opposite continent which surrounded the true ocean.... Now in this island of Atlantis there was a great and wonderful empire...* (Timaeus)*

Atlantis, according to Plato, was the seed civilization of the West, mentored consciously by titans, vast spiritual entities associated with planetary zones. The titan Atlas is a mythic description of the living consciousness of the Atlantic ocean and the land masses that it influences. Atlantis was the first perfected glyphic city, sited on a sacred island in the ocean. More simply, its cosmic archetype was the same as that of the perfected Jerusalem so vividly described by Blake, Swedenborg, and other mystics.

Here we touch upon a distinct esoteric tradition of the glyphic city being prepared in ancestral consciousness through the interaction of early humanity and planetary energies or spiritual entities (such as the titan Atlas, Cronos as described by Hesiod, and the recurring image of Albion in the work of Blake). At this early legendary time, the Fire Temple receives its power from the telluric core, rising through volcanic openings. This is the source of the tradition represented by Empedocles and others. However, the Atlantean culture was destroyed by earthquakes and tidal waves, but not before sending out Seed Bearers to the four planetary directions. The glyphic city, as a spiritual archetype, remains ever present, immanent, ready to manifest given the right conditions.

William Blake mapped this glyphic city onto London, insisting that Jerusalem could be built in Britain: this is a mythic and spiritual theme, with many profound implications. Of course, it applies to any locus, any power place, anywhere on the planet. Hence one of the esoteric insights often stated by ARH that power places are linked together through the center of the earth, a theme that we will explore shortly.

Dion Fortune, The Fire Temple, and the Sea Temple

In the vigorous Glastonbury revival of the early 20th century, we find Dion Fortune writing about the Goddess and the Sea Temple of Atlantis. We find A. R. Heaver mediating the Fire Temple and the *Aesch Mezareph* of prophetic and purifying fire. It is through traditions regarding the center of the Earth and the sacred volcano, prime emblems of Atlantis, that these two streams of Sea and Fire Temple come together. This communion is experienced directly within the Sphere of Art.

Through the Center of the Earth

There were certain themes that ARH initiated, that have evolved in my work over the last 30 and more years. Here are some examples:

1. Spiritual Transformation and the Planet

ARH emphasized that spiritual transformation is not only interior to the human consciousness: its impulses originate in the stellar realms and pass *through* the body of the planet, through its stellar fiery core, to resurface in a new manner. If we are able to attune to this rising light from below, we can benefit from it as a catalyzing and empowering force. This tradition, which I have described in modern terms in several books, reaches far back, and is found most emphatically in the philosophical and cosmological writing of Empedocles (490 BCE -430 BCE)[6]. To work with forces of spiritual transformation to greatest effect, ARH suggested we must follow a similar path into the Earth and back out again. We can see connections here not only the Empedoclean, UnderWorld and folkloric faery traditions, but to the influential Rosicrucian tradition that surfaced and developed in the 16th and 17th centuries in Europe, wherein all the major action took place in a sealed underground vault, aligned to stellar and planetary forces[7]. This mystery of the UnderWorld is an age old tradition, of course, with many variants more ancient than that of Rosicrucianism.

ARH stated that *ley lines* are not "straight paths" as they are typically described, discovered on the surface of the land connecting points or locations, and they are not a network like that of an electrical circuit, which is the most commonly copied analogy. Instead of this simplistic approach, ARH stated that ley lines are angular relationships between forces that pass through the center of the Earth, descending and ascending, entering and emerging at the key locations or points that we can identify (such as churches, temples, wells, springs, standing stones and so forth). Thus a ley line is often threefold, comprising an inward movement of energy down into the earth, an upward movement back to the surface, and the third connection along the surface between them. We are only aware of the surface connection, which we see, with our human interpretation, as a so-called straight line.

ARH also stated that these angular relationships are identical to the aspects of a natal chart: trine, square, sextile, conjunction, opposition, and so forth. This theory raises significant ideas on the relationship between places of power in our world, and offers the possibility of drawing up a three dimensional spherical chart of their interconnection through the planetary core. ARH stated that to make changes in Jerusalem, for example, one had to work with the subtle forces of another power place that had a specific relationship to Jerusalem *through the centre of the Earth*: in this case, he was, of course, referring to Glastonbury.

1a. The Arimathean Tradition, the Tomb, and the Grail

This leads us to the Arimathean tradition of Joseph and Jesus, the root Mystery of a spiritual link between ancient Britain and the Middle East, that was so significant to William Blake and earlier British mystics, all the way back to the Middle Ages. Mediation of the Arimathean Mystery is closely connected to the Rosicrucian Vault mystery, and in some aspects they are deeply intertwined.

In or around 1935, ARH travelled to Jerusalem to visit the Garden Tomb just outside the Damascus Gate in the Muslim quarter. *"As usual, the decision to do anything of this kind always seemed beset with seemingly insurmountable difficulties. However, in all-night silent vigil at Glastonbury my resolution was confirmed and on return to London I booked my passage on the Cunard liner Laconia due to sail from Southampton for Haifa…"* [12]

This sanctuary garden, which had been a vineyard some 2,000 years before, at the time proposed for the life of Christ, contains a crudely extended ancient tomb. A preservation trust was first established by General Gordon in the late 19th century, during his visit to Palestine in 1882-83, and continues to this day. The Garden Tomb is thought by many to be the true site of the tomb of Jesus, given, according to legend, by his uncle Joseph of Arimathea. *"On returning from this memorable visit, I found that Lord Lee of Fareham, a former Civil Lord of the Admiralty who had given "Chequers" to the nation as private residence for prime ministers, had made an appointment to see me at my office. His opening remark "I have just seen the Garden Tomb in Jerusalem. It has the most powerful aura of any place on earth I have ever contacted" made a profound impression on my mind coming as it did from a man of such renowned practical attainments."* [12]. ARH was soon to make a second visit, to negotiate preservation of the part of this ancient site associated with the legend of Golgotha. After months in Jerusalem, his negotiations were successful.

The mysterious Arimathean tradition, connected to that of the re-generative Tomb and the Grail is a fusion of pagan and primal Christian themes. It refers to the theme of the sacred blood and seed, the red and white powers of regenerative spirit, to which we will return shortly[8]. In an alchemical context, there is a deeply significant connection in the Armithean Mystery, for British tradition preserves the story that Joseph brought the boy Jesus to the west of England (Cornwall, Devon, Somerset) on his trading journeys to obtain *tin*. This alchemical connection will be explored more deeply in our volume 2.

The tomb imagery that permeates the Mysteries is more than allegory: it repeatedly arises in connection with an esoteric tradition that stellar spiritual energies become embodied in the planet, revealing how humanity may mediate such energies consciously.

Britain and the Americas

In conversations from ARH, which were protean rather than linear or systematic, the concept of a polar connection, through the heart of the earth, between physical locations, was sometime extended to describe a polar relationship between Britain and the Americas. With regard to the planetary future: "in the past we looked to Tibet for spiritual enlightenment, but in the future it will arise in South America".

With this prophetic statement, I should add that ARH was not espousing the idea of Tibetan or eastern spirituality, but stating that its influx into the western consciousness had formed an essential aspect of the collapsing phase of the British Empire, at a time when exoteric Christianity had cast off all spiritual worth or integrity in exchange for political hypocrisy and material authority. ARH's spiritual practices were firmly founded upon mystical Christianity and the esoteric prophetic (Qabalistic) traditions that underpin Judaism, Christianity, and Islam, rather than upon any eastern philosophy. Furthermore, he made this statement about Tibet and South America not in terms of religious alternatives, but in connection with sacred power mountains, coming awake in the future. In 2005 I found this tradition of the linking of sacred mountains around the world active and reaching out, from shamanistic sources in Peru, exactly as ARH had predicted back in the mid-1970's.

The significant polarity between Britain the Americas and Canada is neither historical accident nor political expediency; it arises from deep within the Atlantic ocean as the influence of the Titan Atlas, spirit mentor of human civilization in the west, as described by Plato. The westward movement of western civilization, often said to be founded by the ancient Greeks, but attributed to ancient Atlantis in tradition, is not mere expansionism. It is a planetary and telluric tide, bringing certain forces into the evolution of human consciousness, and thus, through human influence, into planetary life at large.

The Involutionary and Evolutionary Streams

In later years I realized that with this idea of lines of power passing into and out of the center of the Earth, ARH also described the Twin Streams that flow in and out of our planet: the *involutionary* and *evolutionary* forces that permeate everything, which were typified in the ancient world as underworld rivers, and in bardic druidic tradition as the Red and White Dragons[9]. From this impulse, therefore, came my work with the UnderWorld, which occupied several books such as *The UnderWorld Initiation, Earth Light, Power Within the Land*, and *The Well of Light*. By the time *The Well of Light* was written in 2003, there was a substantial foundation in place, to support this book on *The Sphere of Art*. I should state that all of the above are my own responsibility and original writing, and that any flaws therein are not attributable to either the tradition or to my various mentors.

In several of these books a diagram of the complete Tree of Life is found, which includes an UnderWorld pattern: this is reproduced as our Figure 1. This OverWorld and UnderWorld tree became a feature of my own spiritual life, at a time when it was hardly known in standard Hermetic Qabalah, and often regarded as "dangerous" due to conservative religious ignorance. It was only in retrospect that I discovered its connections to the spiritual forces mediated by the lineage of Zadok, and described in the alchemical text *Aesch Mezareph*, to which we will refer shortly.

In our present context, I will not repeat at length material found in my earlier books unless pertinent to our discussion of the Sphere of Art and the Two Sensitive Points. Table 1 shows the developing sequence and dates of the publications.

2. The Folk Soul of Britain

ARH often referred to his spiritual life as being linked in some mysterious way to what he called "the folk soul of Britain". This theme has played a major part, albeit in a different expression, in my own work in writing, music, and teaching, as I am convinced that all magical and spiritual work must be firmly rooted in the collective ancestral traditions, and that these traditions are, far from being quaint bizarre remnants of bygone days, a powerhouse of spiritual transformation.

Such traditions arise from and obtain power within the Under-World, that regenerative sacred consciousness that we may enter by passing within the body of the land or planet in mediation, vision, and ceremony. This message has now gone out to many students and practitioners of magic, revival paganism, and esoteric spirituality, whereas when I began publication on the theme in the mid- 1970's, it was often regarded with unease and suspicion by both pagans and Hermeticists, due to the severe hangover from Christian propaganda merged with neo-Eastern escapist spirituality that permeated the magical and spiritual revival. The idea of earth magic was concurrently developing in revival paganism and witchcraft, in the 1960's and 1970's, using a mythic sacromagical model of rituals and deities adapted from ancestral tradition. This significant movement, which has done much to transform modern western consciousness, did not have a coherent UnderWorld aspect in its early days, though we see it increasingly appear over time.

Earth-based spirituality is now a very popular phrase, but when *The UnderWorld Initiation* was first circulated then published, in the 1970's and early 1980's, the idea was still startling. It was Gareth Knight, the renowned British Qabalist and occult author, who convinced me that this material should be published…through the justified ploy of sending a copy to a publisher without telling me until it was too late. Without Gareth, *The UnderWorld Initiation* would not have been published at that time, as I originally wrote it for private circulation.

From the mid-1970's onwards, there was a substantial revival of interest in folkloric and mythic themes…the Matter of Britain, not only as literature, but as living spiritual tradition. Gareth played a major role in this, following a powerful initiatory path from clues regarding Arthur and Merlin set out by Dion Fortune. Dion Fortune was a contemporary of ARH, both lived in London and Glastonbury, albeit at varying times, and they had occasional contact.

When I asked ARH if he had known Dion Fortune, he answered "yes, she practiced ritual magic you know" but he felt that ritual magic was "unnecessary" and that much of the art was overly complex and confused. During one conversation, I realized that he found it amusing. ARH was referring, of course, to the top-heavy text and equipment based methods of the 19th century, as the process of simplification and clarification had barely begun in the first half of the 20th century. By the late 1960's and early 1970's Gareth Knight and W. G. Gray, had both, in different ways, begun this process with remarkable new books on magic that disposed of much of the clutter and obscurity. By the middle of the 1980's, I too had followed this path towards clear exposition, in my own books on the art.

It is due to Gareth's pervasive influence that many aspects of the western tradition have opened out and become more available to the general reader, and I owe him much respect for his support of my own work over the years. Following the inspiration of Gareth Knight, John and Caitlin Matthews produced substantial works on the Arthurian themes, and I produced a series of books on the Merlin tradition and the Prophecies of Merlin[19]. Much of our early work was developed during public classes and workshops presided over by Gareth at Hawkwood College, Stroud, England, in the early 1980's. There was also a potent interaction in closed group work, conducted in a private temple sited at my house in Bath, England, within the ancient Romano-Celtic temple precinct. These gatherings were not open to the public.

Another influence on the writers and thinkers who moved in this stream was the late Kathleen Raine, poet and Blake scholar, who had been a member of a magical order in her younger years. During a visit in the late 1980's, she acted as a catalyst, moving me into a new phase of my creative and spiritual work, with just a few words. There was never any small talk or idle conversation at Kathleen's, and she had a habit of cutting right into the spiritual heart of your life. Suddenly she asked me if I was still writing about Merlin, and I replied that I had more or less ceased this task, but might have something for the future. Looking not at me, but through me, to deep within, she said "Arthur and Merlin are all very well as a place to start, but one cannot stay with them forever". These words are significant for us all. This ability to see through a person, to their very depths, was something that ARH also demonstrated: in his presence one felt utterly transparent and open.

Gradually I have come to understand that while Gareth Knight followed on from Dion Fortune, and has continued to the present day to refine and advance the foundations laid down in her remarkable and highly significant work, I have followed, often unwittingly but with growing comprehension, from A. R. Heaver. ARH was not my sole mentor, nor my sole source of inspiration, but the spiritual lineage that he embodied and communicated to me has had a profound effect upon my life. The UnderWorld and Earth Light work, both as published and as taught in public and private, is directly in line with some of the esoteric statements from ARH, albeit developed further through my own practices and insights into the catalytic transformations available when working with the UnderWorld.

The UnderWorld theme and related practices, such as the Threefold Alliance within the faery tradition described in my books, comprise an essential *foundation*, but they are not the *crown*. We need the transformative forces such as the faery realm, the Crossroads, the ancestors, and the titans, to bring us into a state of balance and readiness to work with stellar spiritual influences. At a deeper level this requires that we become aware of the deep roots of the Tree of Life in the UnderWorld, for a tree with shallow roots may grow swiftly up to the light for a season, then it topples over and dies. The Threefold Alliance, of human, faery, and living creature, makes a strong mutually supportive bond, whereby all members are uplifted and transformed together.

Work leading towards the *crown*, supported strongly by that "folk soul" and land-based spiritual foundation, is described in my magical arts books, most recently in *The Spirit Cord*. These all explore the subtle use of energy and working with Inner Contacts in modern sacromagical arts. Elements that appear in all of these books are integrated here, in the practices of *The Sphere of Art*, but the folkloric and earth-based magical aspects are omitted, partly because they are found in the other books, and partly because they are less pertinent to this spiritual path. Nevertheless, we cannot fully operate the Sphere of Art unless we have true experience of the UnderWorld, of the ancestral spiritual traditions, and the related inner contacts from the faery realm. This will become clear in our main chapters, for we actively combine the spiritual forces of the OverWorld and Under-World in the Sphere of Art. This is not a theoretical exercise, or an idealistic meditation, but a vigorous demanding experience.

3. Aesch Mezareph: The Purifying Fire

On ARH's grave there are two quotations, one from Isaiah 40:31. "But they that wait upon the Lord shall renew their strength; they shall mount up with wings as eagles, they shall run, and not be weary". This was his meditation during his pain and disablement. The other is more enigmatic, for it says *Aesch Mezareph*, which means the purifying fire. We might wonder why ARH has this obscure phrase on his tombstone, in the peaceful rural graveyard of Keinton Mandeville church in Somerset. The Aesch Mezareph is a spiritual power, a stellar fire that transforms the Elements. We know that ARH underwent a miraculous healing process, after having been given no more that two days to live, in 1926, as an ongoing result of injuries incurred when his biplane was shot down in the First World War. He describes this as follows: *"I was completely paralyzed, the doctors giving me only forty-eight hours to live. Surviving this crisis, I faced a crisis of confidence when…the king's physician announced bluntly that that I would never walk again…under orthodox treatment I made no progress at all. It was not until I abandoned orthodox treatment entirely that progress moved fast toward recovery"*[12]

My understanding is that the unorthodox healing was through the power of the Aesch Mezareph. One of the key techniques in the Sphere of Art is that of working with Aesch Mezareph contained exclusively within the Sphere. But there is more, for *aesch* is the spiritual fire focused for alchemical transformation. It is a cosmic power (related to the cosmic rays measured by modern science, but of a metaphysical nature) that causes transformation, or more accurately, *evolution* of metals elements or minerals within the mantle of the Earth. Under certain conditions it can accelerate our spiritual evolution: these conditions are created by the Sphere of Art.

Aesch Mezareph is also the name of a Qabalistic and alchemical text, dating from the Middle Ages, according to scholars, written in Hebrew and probably also in Arabic. Only a Latin translation, of the lost Hebrew manuscript, is known today, and English translations depend from this somewhat corrupt but still approachable Latin source. When his grave was inscribed thusly, ARH intended us to look up this source, with which he was more than familiar.

Enter Luis Rota

In the 1950's ARH attempted to bring the work of the French alchemist and alternative scientist Luis Rota (1886-1951) into the energy industry in Britain, to counter the burgeoning development of nuclear generators. This attempt did not succeed, just as early attempts by the British Admiralty to utilize Rota's work were discarded, for reasons that are still unclear. ARH had an ongoing connection with the Admiralty, no doubt starting in his teenage years as a pilot, when he joined the Royal Naval Air Service. In later years this continued, possibly through a mutual spiritual interest (from British Israel) among some of the higher echelons, or through work in international diplomacy, or both.

Luis Rota worked with what he termed the Universal Current which he detected as active under the planetary surface. Rota's current is a manifestation of what I have termed the Earth Light, the power that radiates from the stellar core of our planet. While we explore the Earth Light through our spiritual experiences and techniques, Rota employed the universal current to produce energy, run equipment, transform metals, and act as a healing agency.

Regardless of the model used to describe it, this earth current interacts with the cosmic and stellar forces, and such interaction is described in perennial tradition as the twin streams, typified in spiritual perception and teaching as Evolutionary and Involutionary "rays", as the Rivers of Tears and Blood, and as the White and Red Dragons of ancient bardic tradition. So within the concept of Aesch

Mezareph we have a Fire Temple tradition…in healing, in alchemy, and in the production of earth-current energy as an alternative to standard forms of electrical generation and nuclear power plants[3].

From the perspective of ARH and many of the older generation alchemists and occultists who had been born into the world before the first nuclear tests and before nuclear bombs were dropped on Japan, the nuclear threat was considerably greater than that of physical radiation. It was a spiritual threat, a major disruption of the Inner Planes. Thus the healing alchemical transformation must be one of planetary regeneration, utilizing a *modus operandi* that uplifts our world out of those disruptive currents set in motion by nuclear science and warfare.

ARH was disabled, as mentioned above, in a plane crash, and suffered from this disability of the spine and legs during the early and latter parts of his life: but he was vigorous and active during his adult years, overall leading a life that often sounds like a heroic British novel: aviator, war hero, international traveler and military advisor, in charge of air-raid protection for buildings in the Buckingham Palace area during the Blitz, negotiator in the Middle East, and so forth. He was shot down during the First World War, when only 16, having lied about his age to get into the Royal Naval Air Service: *"Taking to the air as if it were my native element, I made my first solo flight successfully after only three and one-quarter hours of dual instruction…in a dogfight with the "Richthofen circus" in which the odds were seven to one against us, my plane was shot down and crashed within enemy lines. Used a ground target for fourteen machine guns I should have been a sieve, but miraculously emerged from the wreckage unscathed except for one leg which was badly sprained. This was before the days of parachutes, and paralysis as a consequence of the shock to my spine was to develop later"*[12].

This violent fall from the sky is resonant of the myth of Icarus, but more significantly in our British context, of the sacred king Bladud, founder of the sacred healing temple in Bath, who flew through the air on artificial wings, and is traditionally associated with Druidism, magic, and establishing the first universities in Britain[10].

In warfare there are miraculous escapes, but we might feel that ARH was dedicated to a life path that precluded an early death. The curious "immunity" to bullets experienced by ARH was known in the Gaelic faery tradition and examined by English intelligence officers for military purposes in the 17th century[15]. My grandfather, Thomas Stewart, in a Highland regiment in the First World War, received a medal for single handedly storming a German machine gun emplacement that had his men pinned down in a trench. Just as ARH describes, he should have been a sieve, but was untouched. During a conversation with Ed McGaa, a Native American veteran of the Vietnam war, Ed told me that he had flown many missions without once being wounded, and that a protective magic had been placed upon certain warriors that made them immune to bullets. Thus we find this folkloric theme, known from Gaelic tradition in the 17th century, paralleled in Sioux tradition in the 20th: and can cite two historical examples of such immunity during the First World War.

The British Folk Soul, Arthurian and Arimathean Mysteries

ARH's intermittent paralysis was attributed by him, at least in part, to a deep attunement to the British folk soul, a term that he used, and deeply associated the mythos of the wounded Grail king. He also demonstrated that with determination we may cure such paralysis by the art of the Aesch Mezareph, the purifying spiritual fire. Paralysis, disconnection, can be of the spine, the soul, the land, the planet. They are all one. In his latter years, his body progressively becoming immobile again, ARH's role was as a deep mediator of spiritual forces, and it was at this time that I received a specific initiation from him, involving the transmission of the sacred fire, close to the time of his death.

So when we work today with the Sphere of Art and the Two Sensitive Points, these are specialized developments of the art of transformation through the sacred fire, the perennial mystery of Prometheus. Not fire in the service of aggression and militarism, or as a source of profit through unethical technology, but the stellar fire that seeds and stimulates the evolution of consciousness. Under special circumstances this evolutionary impetus can be accelerated. The methods of the Sphere have grown slowly over thirty years, but they connect to a powerful spiritual lineage of which ARH was a senior mediator during his life on Earth. If you are willing to work with this Sphere of Art, you will come into contact with stellar fire temple energies, mediated by Inner Contacts poetically called the lineage of Zadok.

This lineage combines, as ARH himself put it, the Arimathean and the Arthurian Mysteries on earth, that is, in our manifest world of nature: *"It was under the continuing shadow of the thermonuclear stalemate that the Avalon Group came into being. As an organism rather than an organization, this group is dedicated to the task of perpetuating the Arimathean and Arthurian traditions embodying as they do all that the symbol of the Holy Grail inwardly and truly represents. A long-term aim of the Avalon Group is to work for the realization of the vision of William Blake who spoke of building Jerusalem in England's green and pleasant land, a vision which we interpret as meaning the manifestation on earth of the conditions of the plane of divine perfection, made possible as a consequence of the coming regeneration of the whole creation"*[12]

In the Sphere of Art these lineages cease to be mythic or cultural, and appear in their pure forms, as sources of spiritual power, at an originative and creative level beyond that of the ancestral or collective. They fuse together in a new manner, a higher octave of that fusion borne by the Arthurian (faery and UnderWorld) and Arimithean (solar and OverWorld) Mysteries. This fusion is of stellar and telluric fire, creating a New Sun which transforms all things with its radiance. This is a *spiritual fusion*, not a *nuclear fission*. Such was the intention of Alfred Ronald Heaver when he left London in 1959, and moved to Keinton Mandeville: *"discovering an appointed place exactly midway between Glastonbury and Camelot, the geographical centers of the Arimathean and Arthurian traditions respectively. Here a Sanctuary of Avalon was created, dedicated to the power of the Divine Name and set apart for prayer and silent meditation"*[12]

It was in this sanctuary, in the early 1970's, that I came into silent contact with the stellar fire contacts and consciousness that we now access through the Sphere of Art and the Two Sensitive Points. Dion Fortune referred, obliquely, to the Stellar Fire Temple Mystery as the spiritual vessel of the Order of Prometheus, though she seems to have written little else on the subject. Further research into the legend of Prometheus in classical tradition will reveal many themes for contemplation, relating to the fire mysteries in heaven and on earth[11].

If you work with the Sphere of Art, you will come into contact with the spiritual power behind the Avalon Group described by ARH. In recent years the word Avalon has become fashionable, often trivialized, with the continuing exteriorization of the lesser Mysteries. But the greater Mysteries are only perceived in an altered state of consciousness, beyond words, through deep attunement to transhuman awareness: this is enabled by the Sphere of Art.

In 2007 I opened a new Sanctuary of Avalon, in a small building in an apple orchard, just as ARH did some 50 years past. This new sanctuary, attuning to the ancient mystery, is thousands of miles west of Somerset and Glastonbury with their watery rhines and marshes leading to the Severn Sea and the Atlantic. The new Sanctuary is between the redwood forests and the shores of that other great ocean, the Pacific. The primary movement has always been westwards, a planetary surge that has created the all embracing phenomenon of western civilization. In the 1960s ARH wrote: *"My living faith embraces the conviction that the English- speaking peoples acting together in unity have a unique role to play in the service of mankind...".*[12] When I first heard this concept, I thought that it was typical English superiority, such as often formed the basis for imperialistic propaganda. Today, with hindsight, I understand it better. This affirmation from ARH reminds us that the vast financial and military power of the western cultures has the potential to change the world for the better, or to plunge it into endless strife. At this time, in 2007, we teeter at the brink of an abyss of ongoing de-centralized warfare, in which there are no winners, but that compassionate civilization is most likely to lose: the nuclear threat has reasserted itself in many ways from missiles to terrorism…but of course, it never went away. All of this has come about due to the influence of the English speaking races, permeating the planet through capitalism, imperialism, and modernism. The key phrase in ARH's affirmation is *"in service of mankind"*, and beyond and behind that, in service of the living spirit of All Being.

R. J. Stewart, California, 2008

Chapter One
Essential Concepts

The aim of this book, the first of two, is to describe a specific magical method, and to reveal to the reader some of the implications and powerful effects of this method. This is a serious and focused art, unsuitable for complete beginners. We live in a time in which there are an increasing number of dedicated practitioners of sacromagical arts, so there is no discussion of basics here. There is, however, an emphasis on re-assessing deep concepts and powerful practices that are hidden within full view, often within the so-called basics or early stages of magical training. The most advanced magical work is identical to the most basic, but in a different manner, with far-reaching effect. Anyone who expects "advanced" work to be complex and obscure has simply not had sufficient experience, or perhaps has spent too much time reading about magic and not enough time doing it. You should have some hands-on experience in meditation, ceremony, and visualization before you undertake this magical system, with its modular forms[13].

In practice, providing the student has focus and intention, and has undertaken the basics of meditation and magical work, the method described here will substantially open out his or her skills, sensitivity, and higher awareness. In addition the concepts behind this material are most fruitful in meditation, providing a further path of practice that supports and informs ritual work in general, and the practice of the Sphere of Art in particular. While meditation is recommended and deeply beneficial, our work with the Sphere is an ongoing sacromagical process, a simple ceremonial path of transformation, and cannot be undertaken solely as meditation or visual-ization. It must be done, repeatedly, as ritual. Much of this dialectic between meditation/ritual is of course, false. You cannot conduct a ritual without meditation (unless it is an empty social ceremony) and you cannot meditate without some ceremonial component, even in the simple act of sitting or walking during the meditation. Despite the foregoing, there is an increasingly unhealthy emphasis in the contemporary revival of spiritual practices on actions "in the mind" or solely through "journeying" or "path-working". The terms journeying and path-working have been used out of their original contexts so often, that there is little hope of restoring them to their original meaning, one from shamanistic magic, the other from Qaba-listic magic. While the originals were, and still are, dynamic interac-tive experiences requiring strength, discipline, and courage, the popu-larized versions tend be dilutions or simulations of what were once intense highly trained visionary arts, often leading to vague or indul-gent fantasy rather than empowered imagination. The contemporary surge of simulation and obsession with simulacra is prevalent in every aspect of modernist culture, especially on the internet, whereby hu-man consciousness gives itself up to simulation within a machine. The imagination atrophies as a result, and our isolation increases, replac-ing participation in the living world with simulation[16].

Throughout this text you will find occasional recommendations for meditation, which highlight a concept or phrase, and invite the reader to meditate upon it. Initially you should read through the en-tire book before entering into any of the practices, but a brief pause to meditate upon these indicated concepts will be helpful even with your first reading, bearing in mind that they are there to support the main practices, not to replace them.

There are further stages of this work that can only be taught ver-bally, and their effect must be experienced directly in shared prac-tice. These further stages, by their very nature, cannot be described or conveyed directly in text alone. Advanced material is taught to students who have reached a certain level of development through their practices, through a direct transmission and mutual experi-ence within group work. This first book is intended to bring stu-dents, be they long term practitioners or relatively recent, into the methods of the Sphere of Art and the Two Sensitive Points, through *forms* and *practices* that can be undertaken individually or in a small training group. Those wishing to progress to the deeper levels of the work can build their own foundation through the methods described, and become ready to undertake what may follow from direct transmission.

Forms are the units or modules of our art: they may combine many or few skills such as meditation/visualization/ceremony/movement. In the spiritual martial arts or ritual dance, various forms are learned and combined. Typically the forms are handed down within a school or tradition. *Practices* should include the regular rhythmic work done with the various forms, and tend towards an overall path or direction of sacromagical commitment, usually within, but not limited to a tradition. In our present context, *forms* and *practices* both contain new material, developed through contact with a deep sacromagical tradition, expressed in a manner suitable for the 21st century student and practitioner. The concept of modular forms in spiritual practice has always been present, but is frequently buried under verbiage.

First the Sphere of Art, then the Two Sensitive Points

The Sphere of Art is an obvious but much neglected development of the standard Circle (upon the floor or ground) so widely used in ritual magic worldwide, while the *Two Sensitive Points* relate to a little known esoteric art, that of transformation of energy. Much of the practical work with Sphere and points relates to alchemy, though not to the popular idea of alchemy and not to the intellectual or analytic approach to alchemy that has been popular in recent years. We will return to this connection to alchemy, especially esoteric alchemy, again.

The Sphere of Art, while described as a "development", is really an inherent pattern that should be brought into magical practice as early as possible, before the student becomes locked into the idea of the flat plane or the popular notion, widely published, of the magical circle as a barrier, something that supposedly excludes inimical influences or entities, and includes whatever is chosen by the ritualists. The latter concept is immediately exploded by one simple truth: *you cannot exclude anything from your circle if you have some trace of it or fear of it within you.* That trace, that fear, maybe that hidden desire, acts an open door. In basic practice, uninformed by deeper metaphysics, it is usually our companion entities and spirit allies that work on the exclusion so often demanded by emotionally insecure ritualists. In this book, we shall go far beyond this idea of the circle as a prophylactic shape, while not entirely dismissing its basic validity.

Before we go further, some basic concepts must be described, and understood by the reader. If you do not grasp these foundational concepts, the practical work that follows will not reveal its full potential to you. Some readers may have to let go of cherished notions and habituated practices to fully enter into the method offered here.

The Magical Circle, the Sphere of Art, and the Thirteen Extensions

The Magical Circle is always (whether we acknowledge it or not) the flat plane, the mid-plane, of a Sphere. Do not approach this as curious theory or speculation: it is a property of the interaction of consciousness and energy. In other words, it is a property of the cosmos, and of our interaction within the cosmos[14]. As a philosophical subject for our ancestors, it informed their contemplations and provided many insights. We inherit this concept, in the western esoteric traditions, primarily through themes associated with Pythagoras, Empedocles, and Plato, but it has many connections worldwide. How could this not be so? Such traditions describe that which is accessible to all levels of consciousness, from our relative position in the physical world of nature (the sub-lunar realm) to our most advanced and recondite theories of physics and cosmology.

This *relative position* is deeply significant for us: our habitual understanding is based upon standing upon the surface, the land. This is a situation entirely dominated, and enabled, by gravity. Land below, sky above, and a choice of directions to walk. It creates the general illusion of a flat plane, within which our lives arise, occur, and cease. The magical circle aims to focus both attention and energies out of the gravitational time-bound theater of consciousness, and into some other. This other is variously described as the inner planes, the spiritual dimensions, the otherworld and so forth. Yet that description is only a small part of the story: the true aim of sacromagical practice is to open out our relationship to the cosmos. There is little point in opening to subtle dimensions if we force our perceptions of them into the gravitational flatland model. To do so is to replace a habitual illusion with a fantastical delusion. Such is the well known problem with the other worlds described in spiritualism or channeling, for they merely mimic the standard, and severely limited, perceptions of everyday consciousness.

The Sphere of Art opens whenever a magical circle is cast or a single meditation is attempted, but in most cases we remain unaware of its presence. Conscious participation in the Sphere, however, provides remarkable results. From the flat plane, or ground/floor, the Sphere extends equally above and below: thus half of it extends upwards towards the sky and stars, and half downwards into the land and underworld of the planet, as shown in our Figure 2. The height and depth of the Sphere are naturally defined by the circumference of the circle…thus a circle with many people generates a large Sphere, inherently defined and proportioned by the size of the group and the radius of their community circle. A smaller Sphere is defined by a small group or by the individual.

Please note: in individual work the Sphere is naturally compact…we should not seek to extend it in a grandiose manner, as the compact nature of the Sphere enhances its transformative power. Typically, if you stand as, and in, the centre, the individual Sphere extends above your head as far upwards as your extended arm and fingertips can reach, and reaches a similar distance, mirrored below you, as if your body was reversed with your head and arm pointing downwards, and the soles of your feet upwards. Poetically we might say that your underworld feet and your overworld feet touch soles on the level plane of nature. In this basic example, the circumference of the Sphere is double your body length plus the length of your extended arm and hand above your head, in both the upright and inverted or mirrored body. When working with the Sphere, the individual practitioner often stands in the centre, and sequentially in the directions. Group work tends to be located in the Four Directions, with members approaching the center occasionally during any ritual. Both patterns must be practiced and experienced in order to fully develop this art.

The locus where the feet touch the ground, and where the over and underworld soles touch one another, is often where we feel the energy of the planetary field enter our bodies. This perception is enhanced through our exercise *The Rising Light Below* (see appendix 2), which is a helpful training form in itself.

The Fivefold and Sevenfold Natures

In many popular books on magic we are told that magic involves a fivefold nature of humanity as demonstrated in the Pentagram; this perennial and hallowed teaching is often trivialized or misunderstood, and has been passed on as a rote method since at least the Middle Ages. We can trace the fivefold nature as a concept at least as early as the work of Empedocles, deriving from Pythagoras, though both (of course) re-iterated ancient tradition. The fivefold nature of the four Elements and a fifth source/interaction within the cosmos, as described in ancient metaphysical philosophy, is different from the contemporary idea of the pentagram, which has acquired a crust of unquestioned dogma over the years. The fivefold nature model was intended as an aid to philosophical exploration, not as a rubber stamp. In our later developments of the Sphere, we will show how the Pentagram relates in another manner to this work, and this will be developed in volume 2. Our primary method of the Sphere of Art invokes, however, not the Fivefold, but our Sevenfold nature, as shown in Figure 3.

Working with the Sphere triggers (initiates) a highly interactive subtle energetic pattern, which includes the lunar, solar, and stellar centers in the over- and under-world bodies, and the six extensions of Above, Below, E/S/W/N. This pattern expands into an eighteen-fold set of energetic interactions, with the power zones of the body extended towards the Four Directions of East, South, West and North. The eighteenfold set comprises the four zones of the body (feet, loins, heart, head) extended to each of the Four Directions, giving 4x4, plus Above and Below, totaling eighteen energetic interactions.

The ramifications of this expansion relate closely to the mysteries of the Platonic Solids within any given Sphere. You do not need to study the Platonic Solids to practice the Sphere of Art, though you may find them helpful. As always, practice is of greater value than intellectual study, so if you find yourself poring over the Platonic concepts in books and diagrams and forgetting to meditate or engage in ritual, you are on the wrong track. Drawing diagrams of the shapes described here may be helpful, especially in developing the basic relationship through the intellect, but it may ultimately be ignored in favor of the subtle senses and practical work with the Sphere. Spiritual magic is not electronics or computer design. The cosmos continues to function even if we do not map it, and humans so often mistake the map for the journey, the description for the experience. This distinction is crucial to effective magic.

In practice, we do not need to formally or overtly go beyond the Eighteen-fold pattern, with the single and important exception of the spiritual locus in the centre of the Sphere, the core or heart. Even the Eighteen-fold pattern may be too much for some people to hold in their awareness, but the good news is that much of this is done "automatically" or we might prefer to say organically, when we extend our awareness to the Four Directions or Four Segments of the Sphere.

Another helpful way to describe and understand this organic process is that even if you are not holding all eighteen extensions in your full awareness, they are naturally present and varyingly active as a result of your extending consciousness and energy into the Four Directions/Segments of the Sphere. Later in this exposition, and especially in volume two, we will consider the interactions with spiritual beings (in each Segment) that are of such major significance and effect in all magical arts worldwide, regardless of religion or tradition.

The central locus mentioned above can be very small and compact, relating to the feet, or it can expand through three stages, to the Loins, to the Heart, to the Head, to include the body above the mid-plane and its mirrored double below, until its final expansion fills the entire Sphere. Through each stage of expansion, the central locus is equally above and below the plane or circle. We will return to this concept later, but it must be kept firmly in mind at all levels of practice, otherwise we lose our living relationship to the subtle forces within the Sphere. *Meditate upon the Sphere as a volume of concentric spheres*, and you will easily understand this.

If you are familiar with the traditional and Qabalistic/Hermetic attributes of Number, you will observe that the eighteen-fold responses resolve to nine, likewise the 18x3=54, which also resolves to nine. Nine is the number of the Tree of Life from Crown to Foundation, with the 10th Sphere of Kingdom or Completion being the unit of totality, the one that includes all nine, which is both the center and circumference of the Sphere.

The Two Sensitive Points Defined

The Two Sensitive Points are best known in magical arts as general concepts rather than as precise loci for direct magical interactions. In the broadest possible sense they relate to the ideas of "above" and "below" which are found in all metaphysical magical and relativistic models. These prime concepts derive from our living on planet Earth, and give context to our physical movement, consciousness, and relative sense of location. Ultimately we might find something of the sensitive points in the furthest locations that we can conceive and imagine, in the solar system or cosmos, above and below; but there is much more to the sensitive points than a philosophical model of expansion and contraction of imaginative consciousness.

The modes of Above and Below arise as a result of our living in, or rather on, the manifest world, standing, moving, and interacting upon the surface of the earth (which is also the plane or surface of the magical circle); our general perspective is that of sensing the sky to be above and the centre of the planet below. This is, of course, a relativistic illusion: we accept it without thought, and live within it. One of the most remarkable forms of meditation is to liberate to our consciousness from this illusion, as follows:

Consider that there is no Above: there is only Around or the enfolding Sphere of "off-planet", within which the planet has its being. There is no Below: there is only Within or "in-planet", down to the central core of planet Earth where the nearest star still burns, intimately close by cosmic measure, beneath our feet. Make this a daily meditation.

Our "solid Earth" is in fact a mobile mantle in constant motion around a heart of telluric fire. Both Earth and Moon orbit around a locus that is within the planet, just as modern science advises us, restating a truth long known in the magical and spiritual traditions. Earth and Moon are one entity, the Foundation described in Qabalah and traditional mysticism and magic. This concept is of great significance for us in our work with the Sphere, for the energetic and physical sphere of relationship between Moon and Earth, the *sublunar realm*, is the realm immediately prior to manifestation and immediately after de-manifestation of any entity or energy in Nature. Meditation on this concept is helpful.

That which is Above, the enfolding Sphere of all directions off-planet, is also Below on the other side our planet. Furthermore, the relativistic direction of above becomes the Four Directions of east, south, west, and north, when extended to the horizons from wherever we stand. We could say, after only a brief conceptual reassessment, that *all directions are simultaneously above and below or without and within the planet*. Meditation on this concept is helpful.

Planet Earth becomes our reference point, our origin of perception, and our current location for *discovery of the true directions*, rather than a convenient surface upon which linear maps are drawn. This theme is found in primal magical traditions, where a *direction* is not three-dimensional in space, but within consciousness.

To progress in magical transformation and skills, we must strictly expunge our sense of dualism and of potential or actual conflict between above and below. This is not an easy task, as there is a huge inherited burden of conditioning and propaganda from religious dogma, deeply embedded in the collective consciousness, and thriving within the processes of modernism and materialism. *Lower* is considered synonymous with *lesser* or judged to be *negative*, while *higher* is identified with *greater* and judged to be *positive*.

You cannot work effective magic while you are enslaved by these ingrained inaccurate notions, for they keep you trapped in the delusion of a world dominated by gravity and thus severely limited by conditioned dualism. Ongoing rhythmic use of the Sphere of Art and the Two Sensitive Points brings progressive liberation from this trap. We may not free up immediately, but the liberation is surprisingly rapid, providing we repeat the associated Sphere rituals in an ongoing manner. As the rituals themselves are short, most taking only around 15 minutes, this is not a laborious process.

Where Are the Two Sensitive Points?

The Two Sensitive Points are found at the upper and lower extremes of any defined Sphere of Art; if you stand in the center or at the perimeter, they are above your head and beneath your feet, the lower point being one arm's length beyond your mirrored crown below. If the Sphere is larger than that of your body, the sensitive points are correspondingly higher or lower. These two points should not be thought of merely as relativistic notions of above and below, but as precise and active loci involved in the dynamic movement of subtle forces within and without the Sphere. They function as gates or, more precisely, irises that allow energy into or out of the Sphere from above and below. We will return to this concept of the sensitive points as irises and the flow of energy in and out of the Sphere in Chapter Two.

The Pillar and Well of Light and the Sensitive Points

The sensitive points relate broadly to the major concepts of the pillar and well of light discussed elsewhere[15] and found in folkloric magical and formal magical arts and esoteric philosophy. In general practice the pillar of light is understood to be a central power extending infinitely above and below, a theme widely known in metaphysics. It is the Axis Mundi of Renaissance magic and of classical philosophy, the pillar of the worlds that links our Earth and Moon to the Sun, Planets, and Stars, the Middle Pillar of the Tree of Life. In the faery and underworld traditions, the Well of Light, often described as an entrance to the UnderWorld, releases a focused utterance or beam of the inherent spiritual power of the planet, the Earth Light. This light rises from the radiant planetary core towards the stars, and in a more diffuse form is the regenerative power inherent in our planet tending towards expansion and growth.

Thus far, we have merely restated some of the basic concepts in traditional magic through the centuries, for the pillar and well of light are perennial teachings and practices. But use of the Sensitive

Points changes all such general concepts into specific methods, and allows a number of unusual and little-known practices to be brought into effect.

If the Pillar of Light is the energetic connection, a planetary beam between the Earth and the cosmos, and the Well of Light is a conduit through the body of the planet for that same Earth Light, then the Sphere and Sensitive points are ways of defining, refining, and scaling such energies in a precise manner.

The existence of the Two Sensitive Points need not be argued, for the proof of the pudding is in the eating. If you work steadily with the methods described, you will becoming increasingly aware of the sensitive points, and become steadily more proficient in your use of them to change consciousness and attune and enhance subtle forces, both within the Sphere, and within yourself.

We now move to a theme that is vital for this art, and this section should not be passed over, even if you feel that you are familiar with its ideas. Some readers will find cherished notions and practices challenged in what follows.

The Sensitive Points and the Three Extensions Are Not "Chakras"

To get the best results from your work with the Sphere and the Points, you must dispose of any and all chakra systems and practices adopted from neo-Eastern teachings. None of the zones or points in this exposition can be equated in a one-to-one manner with popular chakra teachings, and if you make such an equation, you will confuse your flow of energy, and degenerate your Sphere. As in all spiritual disciplines, the old vaudeville song holds good: "It ain't what you do; it's the way that you do it". A musical analogy could be helpful, for when you play the tuba you do not try to play banjo chords, though both are music, both create sound waves, and both are played by the interaction of consciousness, body, and instrument.

After 40 years of magical practice, I have come to the conclusion that popular chakra teachings are a powerful and possibly intentional blockade against spiritual development. They offer a trite and simplistic approach, which creates a delusion of false knowledge, and thus a barrier to deeper consciousness and changes of subtle energy within the body. Curiously, some of the older generation esotericists and magicians in Britain used to teach that the popular chakra system, more or less standardized in so many books, wall charts, and classes, was intentionally corrupted and confused. This cautionary teaching has been lost in recent years, when many students and self-acclaimed authors and teachers pay lip-service to superficial chakra-dogma without really testing its validity. Another way of understanding this situation is that a collective trend, over the last century and more, has built a *simulation* of chakra "knowledge" that is merely copied without consideration of its origins or deeper effects.

By way of balance, I should add that the chakra systems widely promulgated in the west are not those taught in the secretive initiatory systems of the east, but a confused and simplified variant thereof that appeared primarily out of the Theosophical Society literature in the 19th century, later taken up by both western and eastern practitioners in Europe and America, as something easy to assimilate and teach. One clue towards a reassessment of popular chakra-dogma is that a chakra or wheel was originally (and, in eastern traditions, still is) regarded as a tympanum or responsive organ upon which spirit beings could resonate and so interact with humanity. The awakening of these organs of subtle communication and energy was the task of deities and spirits, not of human solipsism. The late Robert Graves described chakra meditation as a form of "self-abuse", a statement that seems outrageous at first, but on consideration reveals itself as profound. Chakras are not a pseudo-mechanistic or electrical circuit system, but organs of reception and communication. To limit the human being to a neo-materialist power grid of chakras (as we find in most books or teachings) is a serious error. The power zones of the body may include chakras, but are not the chakras themselves.

Let us pause to consider that not all humans are identical: maps of energy patterns in the human body are conceptual models, not literal truths. In many cases they work well, but they should never be taken as dogmatic or scientific absolutes…for such absolutes do not exist. Anyone engaged in spiritual or magical work will make changes in their energy patterns, and the method that we are exploring, using the Sphere and Points, brings into focus our understanding of certain shapes of energy and consciousness and allows them to interact, rather than seeking to build and follow an artificial map of energy points within the body. It is at the point where the artificial map becomes dogma that contemporary chakra teachings become a blockade to true spiritual growth. The human body is not an electrical circuit, any more than the land is a railway network. Both pseudo-scientific models, that of chakras as an electrical circuit, and that of ley lines as a railway-like network, were developed in the 19th century by writers seeking to justify mysticism and magic through materialist science. Now, in the 21st century we have no need, as active magicians, to pay homage to materialism. Spiritual truths cannot be explained by materialist models, though the material world may be understood through spiritual insight. The perceptive reader will see not only the simplistic "circuitry" model, but the undoubted connection that chakra dogma has to the drug culture of the late 1960's, and the related bliss culture of hedonistic spirituality.

By allowing *interaction* during our sacro-magical work, and through not attempting to concentrate directly on the presumed chakras themselves, we come closer to the old yogic tradition of the internal subtle timpani (chakras or wheels) as organs of communication between humanity and the cosmos. Thereby we pull away from the neo-materialist solipsist and narcissistic concept of our bodies containing an unrealized energy grid that, if only we could link it all up, would blow the tops of our heads off and bootstrap us into unlimited bliss.

Working With the Two Sensitive Points

The sensitive points are above the head and below the feet. They are not part of our individual psychic or spiritual organism, but are loci that assemble naturally when we create the Sphere of Art. There is, of course, a human component to the subtle forces of the points, but they are not active and present in everyone: they have to be developed. Once you have developed the sensitive points, they may continue to work for you quietly in the background of consciousness, but this stage takes practice and regular repetition. Our concern, in this text, is the interaction of the Two Sensitive Points within the Sphere of Art as a specialized discipline, intended for fully conscious and intentional sacromagical work, and not as a background process.

We should not, therefore, seek to work with the sensitive points without the necessary Sphere training and practice. The Sphere contains and amplifies energy, while the sensitive points release and attract both subtle energies and streams of attuned consciousness into and out of the Sphere. There are risks inherent in attempting to open the sensitive points without the containing and modulating vessel of the Sphere.

The points are always worked in polarity with one another, never singly. We may focus on the point below, for example, but before doing so we will have established both points in the Sphere. The polarity, the interaction, between the points is essential for our method.

Many of the functions of the sensitive points occur naturally, and we do not, and should not, consciously steer or control them. By letting our awareness, imagination, and intention touch them, or "rest upon" them, in traditional terminology, we can interact with the sensitive points. This is a very light and sensitive process, like the brush of feather or a blade of grass, and is not a muscular act of ego or pseudo-will.

The Sphere of Art in Basic Training

The Sphere can be developed and experienced without touching upon the sensitive points of above and below. Indeed, part of our basic training must be to develop skill with the Sphere before we progress to the sensitive points. The aim of our work with the Sphere, however, is to strengthen the Sphere itself, and then open the sensitive points. Only when the Sphere of Art and the Two Sensitive Points are fully active, can we achieve the deeper transformations possible through this unique method.

Always remember that the circle, widely used in magical arts, is only a flat expression of a sphere. Even in standard magical rituals from established traditions that emphasize the circle as a flat working-ground or dedicated space, the subtle forces interact in a sphere, regardless of the awareness of the participants. Other widely taught metaphysical shapes include the cube within the sphere, one of the primary Platonic solids[17]. The interaction between such "solids" (which are not, in fact, solid but interactive, energetic shapes) and the Sphere, is one of our most ancient and powerful esoteric traditions, little practiced today, and seldom understood. An intellectual appreciation and understanding of solid geometry is not the same as the sacromagical application of that geometry to transformation of energy, consciousness, and form.

Once you have begun on this path of initiatory transformation with the Sphere and the points, all your meditations and ceremonies should be conceived of, and practiced within, the Sphere. Not all will involve the sensitive points, and many will not involve the more esoteric Sphere practices, but the basis of the Sphere should inform and support everything that you do in your spiritual life. At a certain stage it will come into full play in your overall life, usually after a period of time, but do not rush this development, which has to happen naturally, like the opening of a flower bud.

The development of the Sphere, the relationship to the Two Sensitive Points, has a deeply transformative effect upon the death and rebirth processes. We will explore this theme again, especially in volume two.

Building the Sphere

The Sphere of Art must be created in specific stages, with no omissions. These stages are itemized later in this chapter, but before attempting them, we must be familiar with the concepts involved. Unless we understand the basic concepts of the Sphere the stages will be merely a checklist, whereas building the Sphere is a creative process far beyond that of simplistic systematic construction. Once we have established our skill at such creation, the process accelerates. An experienced creator of the Sphere will seem to open it instantly; this stage comes after much practice. Once again, the analogy with music, painting, or any other artistic craft holds good: the many hours of painstaking step-by-step practice eventually coalesce into one swift creative flow. As with many sacromagical skills, our assembly of the Sphere accelerates exponentially. The first few efforts may be slow or even clumsy, but once we have experienced the process, and especially after the Sphere begins to come alive and resonate for us, subsequent workings become increasingly rapid and easy.

Our development of the Sphere is more than a matter of personal expertise and experience. In an artistic craft, such as woodcarving, the skill rests with the carver, and the wood takes shape; but there is also an interaction between the carver and the wood that plays a substantial role in the final product. This interaction defines the difference between a simple product and a work of art.

In assembling the Sphere of Art, such interaction is intense and subtly transformative. The Sphere is both Energy and Consciousness, and can never be mere product. While artistic skills tend to be developed from innate talents, and many people may feel that they do not have such talents, magical skills have a very different genesis, for everyone has inherent magical ability. Once we start ("start" is the true meaning of the much abused word "initiate") *the practice of magical arts transforms and expands our ability to practice those same arts.* The more that you do, the more you are able to do. Meditation on this concept is helpful.

The Sphere is not solely built by humans, for it is a co-operative task, shared by spiritual entities that work with us in metaphysical dimensions; with dedication and repetition it takes on a subtle life of its own. Thus the possible interactions are numerous, and we do not undertake the advanced aspects of the work alone. There is a substantial human role in the building of the Sphere, without which nothing can happen. We should focus mainly upon this, our human role, and must be skilled at it before the subtle interactions with spiritual beings can become effective.

Building and working with the Sphere is therefore, a spiritual responsibility, and not a matter of "self-development". The idea of self-development, much touted in New Age literature, is often narcissistic, and may even be damaging to the inner spiritual life in circumstances where egocentric development is confused with spiritual growth. Many intersections of selfish materialism and pseudo-spiritual practices have arisen in the last few decades.

Physical and Metaphysical Temples

There is a much quoted phrase regarding "the Temple not built by hands"…the spiritual temple that is not merely a building, but the hidden truth that any dedicated temple building, or even a simple room, supposedly embodies. With the Sphere of Art we move into a new octave of this truth…for we *begin* with a metaphysical temple (the Sphere) and the physical space is no longer a symbolic statement of spirit or an iconic zone. *As we move into this higher octave, the dedicated physical space empties, and becomes a simple ground without symbolic content.* Meditation on this concept is helpful.

In practice the physical space could be anywhere, but if it is dedicated for regular work it must be plain with minimal content: a bare empty room is best if working indoors, or a clear quiet space outdoors. Outdoor work, absolutely essential for many forms of Earth based spiritual magic, poses some difficulties for long term work with the Sphere. For example, we cannot ensure silence or limit human interaction at an outdoor site. The Sphere of Art is a temple tradition, which is to say it is upheld in a dedicated defined space devoted solely to sacromagical processes, and nothing else. An indoor dedicated space should be white, and have no colors that will polarize either energy or consciousness. In some ritual work with the Sphere, color may be introduced, employed, and then removed, as necessary.

Within the active Sphere, which is already a temple not built by hands, we move to another metaphysical locus, wherein the transcendent becomes immanent, through our communion with spiritual presence, and associated inner contacts. Who and what these beings, these inner contacts are, will be explored later; the significance of the Sphere of Art is that it enables certain forms of consciousness and certain specific spiritual entities to draw close to human consciousness, while excluding others.

Likewise the Sphere enables certain subtle energies to draw close to one another and interact while excluding others. The connection to alchemy is paramount: alchemical operations are conducted in a sealed vessel, enabling, through subtle gradations of Fire, interactions between the contents that might not otherwise occur. Such interactions relate, harmonically, to those that occur in Nature, but are of a different octave. The perfection or evolution of metals, a central theme in alchemy, can only occur naturally in the enfolding transformative vessel of the planet, underground, *before the touch of sunlight or moonlight.* This mystery is known the folkloric faery tradition, for the faery realm is said to be lit by starlight only, having no light from the Sun or Moon.[8]

Once elements are brought to the surface, they interact under the light of Moon and Sun, in the standard manner known to science. The perfection or evolution described in alchemy is attempted by creating a sealed vessel in the alchemical laboratory, which replicates conditions underground, where the telluric fire and spiritual forces of the planet act upon the elements. But there is more, for that which is underground or in a leaden vessel is susceptible to certain cosmic forces, which radiate into the planet when those of the solar system are filtered out.

A similar process occurs in the evolution, or transmutation, of the human being. Over many lifetimes, we are transformed. The period between death and rebirth corresponds to that of the elements or metals deep in the earth, removed from sunlight and the forces of the sub-lunar world of nature, whereby stellar and telluric energies act to bring change in a manner not known to materialist science. In the Sphere of Art we create such conditions in miniature, enabling an alchemical transformation while still in the conscious life: the elements that transform are those within us as incarnate humans. Repeated work within the Sphere, and with the sensitive points, accelerates the distillation processes of wisdom and understanding that normally occur between death and rebirth. Further processes are possible, for the Sphere also opens out our communion with spiritual consciousness while in the human body. Never think of these processes as symbolic or psychological, for if you do so, your work with the Sphere of Art will fail.

The Stages of Construction

There are 13 primary stages of opening the Sphere of Art, and a further nine stages to concluding the work. While this may seem daunting at first, they can each be achieved in a few moments with practice, and the entire process begins to flow rapidly. Indeed, once you have opened the Sphere a few times, you will find that the stages begin to work organically and spontaneously, and need not be steered or enabled through will. The Sphere of Art is a magical process of participation and co-operation, rather than a pseudo-muscular act of will. Some thoughts on the popular idea of "will power" should be explored before we go further.

Exerting will-power in magic is highly over-rated: we would be better exerting the will upon our own limitations and indulgences, and clearing them up before we begin any magical work. Most powerful magic involves not willing things to be, but *allowing them to be what they already are*. This process of allowing is not easily understood, for if it is assessed by the mind alone, it creates a minor paradox. The mind has to be stilled, the will set at peace, within conditions of attuned energy. Not as a meditative process alone, for this is merely preliminary training, but as a sacromagical process that uplifts our manifest creation into another octave of being. Only when we allow this do we discover that there is no paradox and that the other octave of being has always resonated and interleaved with our manifest nature. After meditation upon this concept we can progress to the thirteen simple stages of building the Sphere of Art.

The Stages of Building the Sphere

1 Define the size of the Sphere: individual or group.

Typically members will be just inside the perimeter of the Sphere, aligned to the four planetary directions of east south west and north. The circle is the flat plane of the Sphere, defining its maximum size in all directions. In group work each member must be aware of the direction behind them, before them, to the right and to the left. There must be no ambiguity or uncertainty over which Direction you are in: do not be concerned about degrees of the flat circle or cross-quarters…these will take care of themselves naturally. In advanced work with the Sphere the "cross-quarters" are occupied by spiritual/metaphysical beings, and this is described further in Volume 2.

The floor circle must be as clear and empty as possible. Standard magical equipment should be removed. An empty space is the aim of this art, and less is always more. There is a further aspect of this emptiness to consider, for the spiritual forces of the Sphere will tend to wipe clean most standard magical equipment, talismans, amulets, jewelry and so forth. Be warned: leave all such things outside the Sphere, outside the room. You may wear them again after your working, though increasingly you will find that you do not need them.

In individual work you may also stand in the centre of the Sphere, or sit on the floor, but not in a chair, as this will obstruct. Where a candle flame in the center is referred to in our text, you may substitute your body. Individual work should be done both at the center and circumference. In group work the center is reserved for a flame, a vessel of water, or other (minimal) dedicated objects. Many aspects of working with elements or objects within the center of the Sphere will be discussed in Volume 2. Typically an altar is not used in the center, and items are placed on the floor. However, a simple moveable altar (free of all objects, decorations and colors other than white) can be kept in one of the directions, and placed in the center as required.

2 *Clear and Still the physical working space,* stilling Time, Space, and Movement/Energy. (Use the *Stillness Form*, Appendix Three)

3 *Establish the Directions:* Above, Below, East, South, West, North, Centre.

4 *Clear and Still the Sphere from within the Sphere,* either at the center or at a location on the circumference. From this point all work is undertaken inside the Sphere. In group work, all members work on stilling Time Space and Movement.

5 *Acknowledge the Sensitive Points above and below.* Do not focus on them or open them at this stage. If you sense spontaneous reaction from the Sensitive Points, simply acknowledge this and let it occur, do not follow it or seek to open them out further.

6 *Attune the spiritual energies* of the Four Directions and Centre. *Work with the primary spiritual forces only* as follows: air/fire/water/earth, life/light/love/law, inspiration/illumination/transmission/manifestation and so forth. Do not invoke deities or ancestral or nature spirits, and if habitual magical actions arise for you, still yourself and move through them towards the primary four powers only.

7 *If required light a candle flame in the Center,* otherwise acknowledge and briefly commune with the Center.

8 *Invoke the presence of the Four Archangels:* Raphael/East, Michael/South, Gabriel/West, and Auriel/North.

9 *Build and respond to their Sixfold Wings* that embrace the Sphere*. One pair of wings extends upwards, one pair extends downwards, and one pair extends horizontally to right and left.

10 *Invite the Archangels to Seal the Sphere*.*

11 *Open the Sensitive Point Below:* Earth Light rises to the centre of the Sphere*.

12 *Open the Sensitive Point Above:* Star Fire descends to the centre of the Sphere*.

13 *A New Sun is born in the Sphere,* where the ascending and descending fires coalesce and expand*.

Stages 9-13, marked with asterisks, each have further expositions which follow shortly.

The Mid-Point

By stage 13, we have reached the mid-point of the basic Sphere ritual. You should practice 1-13 as a sacromagical form in its own right. At first the opening out will require focus on each stage. Stages 9-13, marked with asterisks, each have further expositions which follow shortly. With practice the 13 primary stages will open out smoothly and rapidly, culminating in the New Sun in the centre. When we practice this as itself, as a *form*, we then commune in Silence with the spiritual power of the New Sun in the centre, and proceed as follows:

14 *Silent Communion*

15 *Close the Sensitive Points Above and Below*

16 *Invite the Archangels to open and release the Sphere*

17 *Send the accumulated spiritual power out unconditionally,* to the planetary directions in the world of nature, the sub-lunar world

18 *Give thanks and acknowledgment* to those who have worked with us

19 *Re-affirm the seven directions and the centre*

20 *Enter into Stillness*

21 *Extinguish candle flame*

22 *Cause the Sphere to fade, and leave the working space*

Stages 9-13 Expanded

9 The Sixfold Wings. In contemporary usage, archangels are usually imagined as humanoid figures with robes, one pair of wings, and certain implements or symbolic associations. In our practice we return to an older image of archangels having three pairs of wings.

You may conceive of each archangel as humanoid, if you wish. The esoteric, lesser known, image is that each archangel is a Face that utters six wings around it…one pair reaching up to the sensitive point above, one pair to the sensitive point below, and one pair extending horizontally around the circumference of the Sphere.

The tips of archangelic wings all touch, Above, Below, and Encircling. Our meditation here is that the enfolding wings sculpt the Sphere of Art, embrace and define the irises of the Sensitive Points, and enclose the perimeter of the Sphere as follows:

10 The Archangels seal the Sphere. This stage is essential to the operation, and must not be passed over or treated lightly. As with all of the stages, you should practice your sense of this repeatedly until you can feel it clearly.

10.1 Sense, see, and feel the Archangels in the Four Directions. If you are working alone, you may stand in the center, or in one of the Directions. In group work, the members in each direction are responsible for attuning to the Archangel *behind* them. In stage eight we invoke or invite the presence of Raphael, Michael, Gabriel, and Auriel, but in stage 10 we feel their presence behind us, before us, to our right and to our left.

10.2 Wordlessly invite the Archangel behind you to draw close: feel it touch your back. If you are working alone, this invitation will cause all four to draw in equally to the perimeter of the Sphere in the Four Directions with the Archangel behind you touching your spine. In group work you should focus mainly on the direction and Archangel behind you.

10.3 Become aware that the Archangels seal the Sphere by enfolding it with their wings and drawing in close. You do not invoke this, or attempt to steer it in any way. You invite this, and feel it build. To allow this closure of the Sphere, make yourself as still as possible, stilling Time Space and Movement, breathing quietly in and out, and feel the presence behind you and around you.

Note: in standard magical practice the Archangels are invited to bring certain forces into the circle/Sphere, and this is the basis of all attuned work with angelic entities of any kind, for they mediate energy and entities according to their nature and their function upon the Tree of Life. However, the process whereby the Archangels mediate forces into a defined zone is the same process whereby they may seal that zone and exclude any movement in and out from the Four Directions. This is done by the Archangels, not the humans in the Sphere. It is an unusual and little-practiced aspect of the relationship between human and archangel in sacromagical ritual. The aim is that the Archangels exclude all sub-lunar forces from the Sphere.

We cannot say much more in mere words, for you have to open out this relationship and experience it. If you do it, as described, it always works. The more you practice it, the stronger it becomes. This is not a matter of belief, but of training and expertise. Nor is it a matter of faith, visualization, or any of the typical ideas associated with invocation and supplication. None of these things matter, and none of them will work in this context, as they will just interfere with the process. Allow the archangels to understand your invitation by being still, and by feeling the Archangel behind you. When you feel this presence, invite it to draw close and seal the Sphere. Typically we feel them touch our lower back, and often the entire back of the body with a defined current of energy. Each Archangel feels different. If you are working on your own you must practice in the center, and in each of the directions, until you are familiar with all the subtle sensations.

11 The Sensitive Point below is invited to open first. You do not invoke or command, you *let your awareness rest upon the iris below.* As mentioned earlier in our text, this is a light touch like that of a feather. By touching the iris, and sensing the Earth Light beneath it, you will cause it to open. It has already been defined by the wing tips of the Archangels, embracing the point, the opening. Thus there are three components: archangelic, human, and telluric (the Earth Light itself). You may find that the iris opens earlier, but usually it responds to that light touch of consciousness.

11.1 The Earth Light rises into the Sphere. You should be practiced in the Rising Light form through your body, and in the Well of Light practices[15], as this training will enable you to sense, see, and feel the Earth Light. Once again, do not invoke, but participate and acknowledge.

12 The Sensitive Point above is invited to open. You direct your awareness to that point, and touch it. The three components are arch-

angelic, human, and stellar. The stellar component includes a stream of transhuman consciousness, the highly focused inner contacts of the stellar Fire Temple.

13 The New Sun radiates in the center of the Sphere. This is felt with the front of our bodies, just as the Archangel behind you is felt with your back. The entire surface of the body is a sensitive organ, and all four zones respond to this fusion of telluric and stellar energy. If there is a focus in the center, such as an altar or an object, the New Sun will charge it with its power.

The closing phases are also invitations, not commands. The puerile notion of "commanding" archangels to do our bidding plays no part in true magic. You will feel the Archangelic presence ease back to open the Sphere, and the sensitive points fade and close accordingly.

Chapter Two
The Two Sensitive Points

What Are the Two Sensitive Points?

When we have developed our skills, we will soon find that we do not separate the operation of the Sphere and the sensitive points, and that they resonate together, a living pattern of dynamic energy and consciousness. In discussing theory and in early practice, it is helpful to separate Sphere and points to a certain extent, especially as our skills with the Sphere must be established before we can work with the sensitive points. Thus we can, and should, build the Sphere in its own right and then allow the sensitive points to open. There is a temporal sequence in this, due to the laws of the world in which we live.

We should not work with the sensitive points in isolation from, or outside of, the Sphere. This would create an imbalanced and potentially dangerous situation, as the Sphere is the safe vessel within which the sensitive points open. Many cases of challenging "illnesses" or "conditions" such as various forms of autism and schizophrenia may be attributed, subject to further spiritual research, to a condition of random sensitive points in highly impressionable individuals currently coming into this world. Whether or not such conditions embody imbalance or a new mode of human consciousness coming into birth, remains to be seen over time. Much of the apparent problem with such conditions is cultural, for a post-Christian materialistic society combines fear of the unknown with rigid demands upon the known.

In our Chapter One, we described the sensitive points as irises or portals, which can open or close. One is above, one below, at the upper and lowermost extreme of the Sphere. The upper sensitive point opens to metaphysical forces and dimensions with an inherently stellar nature, while the lower sensitive point opens to the metaphysical forces of the Earth Light, the radiant stellar power at the heart of our planet. Note that both sensitive points admit *stellar* forces into the Sphere, thereby enabling and focusing an interaction that seldom occurs in nature. This interaction is a *spiritual octave* of the interaction between the elements within the body of the planet and those cosmic forces, defined by our contemporary science as cosmic rays, that penetrate the earth from deep space. The vocabulary and models of physics and metaphysics may differ, but the basic concepts are often the same.

We need not indulge in popular reductionism to justify spiritual tradition: the metaphysical teachings have been known for thousands of years, while the contemporary models in physics are parallels or alternatives finally appearing within a materialistic mindset. Modern quantum mechanics, often used frivolously and fashionably to justify spiritual or magical concepts, may be seen in the future as nothing more than abstruse bean-counting, for it arrives at conclusions that have been openly available for many centuries in the metaphysical traditions, but reaches them through theoretical models or computerized mathematics rather than through higher perception. If we repeatedly abrogate our higher perceptions in favor of machine derived calculation, they atrophy. Nevertheless we live in a time when a standard dictionary definition states: *"Quantum mechanics suggests that the behavior of matter and energy is inherently probabilistic and that the effect of the observer on the physical system being observed must be understood as a part of that system."* [20]. We will return to this concept in Chapter Three, when we explore the ethical condition of the observer, not in terms of neutral experiment, but in participation.

Evolution of the Elements

In alchemical tradition an evolution of the metallic elements was posited: crudely summarized as from lead towards silver and gold, occurring in a hidden manner within the body of the earth, initiated by mysterious stellar influences. The elements relate to the planets of the solar system, Lead to Saturn, Gold to the Sun, and so forth. We might modify this statement and say that certain elements are fixed by the mediation of their associated planets, but rendered malleable and transformed by the mediation of other planets. What the planets mediate are solar and cosmic subtle forces: these are the Spheres of the Tree of Life that are embodied by the planets of the solar system, and by the elements in the body of Earth. This three-fold mediation and embodiment is present in all forms on Earth, all forms throughout the cosmos.

When the elements are brought to the surface, according to al-chemical tradition, the subtle evolutionary forces cease to interact, and only basic metallurgy is possible using earthly fire. The alchemi-cal vessel and the use of solar and organic heat aimed to re-create the conditions within the body of the planet in miniature. This evolution continues into harmonics beyond gold, of course, and can be under-stood more readily by contemplating the UnderWorld Tree of Life in association with the better known OverWorld Tree. Such contempla-tion of the whole Tree is an essential ongoing meditation, and will greatly enhance your work with the Sphere and the sensitive points.

Sadly, alchemy has become pyschologized in recent years, by people with intelligence but minimal understanding. A psychologi-cal approach to alchemy may help to redeem the weaknesses of psy-chology, but it does nothing for our understanding of the alchemical tradition, which was never a crude proto-psychology, but a highly sophisticated and artistic spiritual science. That which is found in the elements in the Earth, is found in the human body. That which is found in the human body is found in the spiritual or subtle body. This is the traditional teaching that conceals, openly, some astonish-ing methods of transformation. With our operation of the Sphere of Art and the Two Sensitive Points, we can open out a new phase of this perennial teaching apt for the 21st century.

The Directions Compared to the Sensitive Points

In standard magical arts, influences, energies, entities, are in-voked according to the four planetary directions on the horizontal plane, and above and below on the vertical plane. This established method, though taken for granted, can be somewhat misleading, as the "horizontal" directions are never truly flat (nothing is flat, not even the concept of "flatness"). The horizontal directions extend upwards and downwards, as segments of a sphere, merging at the points of Above and Below. This developed understanding of the directions (E/S/W/N) as segments of a sphere must be explored in conceptual meditation, and not merely grasped in the intellect or through drawing illustrations. Meditation upon this brings significant liberation of awareness.

In classic magical arts energetic gateways are typically created in one or more of the directions, and/or in the centre. Such gateways are often formed around an altar, and may be mediated by human participants. All of this is standard practice, and relatively well-known[13]. In advanced and ongoing magical arts, this standard practice requires radical reassessment in terms of the Sphere…but such reassessment is a natural next step rather than a departure from the norm. Indeed, the normative models in magical arts, widely published and practiced, are nothing more than reductions of a spherical model, so working with extensions is neither daunting nor difficult. We live in this spherical condition already, but inhibiting conventions, laid down by subtle religious programming regarding "reality", have reduced our perceptions to random notions fluctuating within a field of conditioned reflexes. When you move to the east, you are extending the eastern segment of your Sphere of consciousness: if you follow this idea in meditation, and consider what may occur for the rest of the Sphere, your conditioned sense of direction, of the world, of the cosmos, will change and grow considerably.

The sensitive points work in a different manner to directional gates and energetic openings at loci or altars. Directional gates open to planetary, spiritual, mythic, ancestral and elemental powers, allowing subtle forces and entities to come into the sphere/circle, and thus to interact with humanity through the magician, priests, priestesses. This is well described in the standard arts of invocation, evocation, and mediation, all of which are enabled by *conscious participation*, through human interaction with the directions and associated subtle forces. Conscious participation is the core of all sacromagical practices, but we have to decide what may be included and what may not. This is the derivation of the hoary old dogma regarding the protective aspects of the circle such as "cast a circle of protection about you!" This last concept is more typical of politicians than true magicians.

The Two Sensitive Points come into effect primarily through the *exclusion* of many powers and entities, and are opened not by invocation or visualization, but by creating a void or emptiness within the Sphere of Art. Only when a certain degree of emptiness has been achieved will the sensitive points open out, and they open out in a spontaneous manner rather than as a result of our concentration upon them. They do not interact with the four directions in the accustomed manner that we use in magical arts, but *respond to their absence*. Working with the sensitive points comprises a Shortened Way. Such Shortened Ways are occasionally mentioned in metaphysical or esoteric literature, but are seldom fully described.

The Shortened Way

Typically a Shortened Way is a cathartic initiatory experience, enshrined within and empowered by, a folkloric magical path or the esoteric teachings of a spiritual tradition. Such methods are known in Zen or Tibetan Buddhism, and these have received attention in western publication. Less well known are the Shortened Ways of the faery and UnderWorld traditions in western and northern cultures, and the powerful initiatory methods hidden within the western Hermetic and alchemical spiritual traditions. It is to these interlaced western sources that we owe the art of working with the two sensitive points, though this art is not found clearly described in standard publications. Some historical alchemical and ritual texts, however, contain this art, in an obscure manner. It is repeatedly stated, though often ignored, that deeper teaching was given orally to support the hints of the texts, as this has always been the traditional method. As time flows, and human consciousness changes, that which was oral and secret gradually becomes written and available: when this change is complete, a new octave of oral transmission becomes available to us, that we may become ready for deeper transformations yet.

With our exposition of the Sphere of Art, we move an (originally) oral exposition into a relatively simple modern text, but still reserve a further level of both new and traditional oral teaching and transmission for the advanced stages beyond our current text. This is, of course, an evolutionary process, for new developments in any art or science must naturally rest upon that which has gone before. Without context we cannot fully engage in anything: in magical arts the context has often seemed to be textual, when in truth it is traditional. The various magical traditions are our context, and texts themselves, ancient or modern, are merely clues towards our interpretation and activation of the teachings and methods found in tradition.

A historian of spiritual practices might see the ongoing operation of the Sensitive Points as an evolved form of *via negativa*, for by defining and establishing that which is *not present* in the Sphere of Art, we discover that which *may become present* when all else has been set aside. Rather than a contemplative long-term method, this is a sacromagical art, effective primarily through ritual, with eminently practical methods and direct physical results that can be felt, discerned, and experienced promptly, hence the potential as a Shortened Way.

But what, we may ask, do we exclude from the Sphere, and why would we exclude it? The answer to this central question is found in our relationship to the sub-lunar realm, and we must explore the implications of this relationship before we proceed further.

The Sphere of Art and the Sub-lunar Realm

The first function and purpose of the Sphere of Art is to exclude the subtle forces of the sub-lunar realm. There are subsequent higher functions, but these will not be active or available to us without the first. By excluding the subtle forces of the sub-lunar realm, the Sphere enables a shortened way both *through* and *between* the Two Sensitive Points, that by-passes the normal convolutions of the sub-lunar realm, and creates a direct interaction between the forces that enter the Sphere from above and below. To grasp both the operation and implications of this, we need first to explore the nature of the sub-lunar realm, and discover why we might choose to exclude its subtle energies for specific sacromagical purposes[9].

The sub-lunar realm is that sphere of subtle forces surrounding planet Earth, which is defined by the rotation of the Moon. Typically we think of the Moon in orbit around the Earth: if we draw a simple diagram of this movement, it looks like a ball of string, with many varied intersecting patterns due to the rapid movement and variations of the lunar orbit. More subtly, this motion is *mutual.* Both Earth and Moon are mutually relating, rotating and orbiting around a locus, the barycenter, deep within the body of the planet. This is a fruitful subject for meditation.

In ancient metaphysics and philosophy, the Earth and Moon were understood to be one single entity: this entity is the Foundation (9th Sphere) described in standard Qabalistic texts, while the 10th Sphere is not only our manifest planet Earth, but the manifest cosmos[18]. To work effective magic we must understand that the manifest Earth, the natural world that we inhabit, is *inside* the Moon, always within that sphere described by the orbiting satellite. Modern geophysics and astronomy make similar statements, describing Earth and Moon as one entity.

In Renaissance magic, drawing upon the traditions of the ancient world, the sub-lunar realm played a prominent role. Today it is either ignored or simplistically brushed-off as being something vaguely to do with the "unconscious" mind or the "dream life". This absence of attention to the sub-lunar realm in 19th and 20th century literature on magical arts is astonishing; it demonstrates the influence of materialist psychology on writers during this period, plus, as always in occult and magical literature, a strong market-driven copyist tendency combined with lack of actual practice. Yet there is a strong insight here: modern society has lost its foundation in so many ways, struggling with aimlessness and hungry materialism that can never sate our needs. At the same time, magical and esoteric literature has lost site of the foundation of much effective magic, found in our relationship to the sub-lunar realm.

The content of popular occult literature, drawing on sources repeatedly copied with minor variations from the 19th century to the present is somewhat like having a powerful vehicle bequeathed to you, but without the ignition key: the ignition is present, but you do not know about it. You can describe the vehicle, sit in it, admire it, repeatedly clean and polish it, but it will go nowhere. Except, perhaps, to roll downhill and then stand still again.

Understanding of, and operation within, the sub-lunar realm is essential to all practical magic. If you do not understand how this realm works, your magical efforts may or may not be effective, and even the effective efforts will vary, instance by instance. Science has recently "discovered" that the repeatable experiment, consistent in result, is an illusion, and this discovery has ushered in a new age of physics. Practitioners of magic have long known this truth, though it is often absent from modern expositions. The ongoing variation in "results" is often due to the consciousness and the ethical condition of the experimenter, but it is also due to the tidal nature and eddies and vortices of the sub-lunar forces which have a persistent tendency to wash all things to and fro and redistribute them. *If we ignore the influences of the sub-lunar realm, we are failing in our responsibility as 21*ˢᵗ *century magicians restoring and regenerating the art to new levels.*

Two Established Modes of Working with the Sub-lunar Realm

Therefore, we may perceive two significant modes of sacromagical work, in any tradition. The first, by far the most common worldwide, seeks to influence the sub-lunar tides and currents from within. This is usually accomplished with the aid of spirit beings that swim, so to speak, within those tides. Indeed, it may not be accomplished otherwise, as a human imprint alone into the sub-lunar realm will soon be washed away and recycled: the human imprint needs to be reinforced, supported, and transmitted. Such spirit beings are, in most instances, cultural, be they found in formal religion or folkloric magic. Folkloric magic works with ancestors, communicating tribal or regional spirits, the faery races, and so forth. Religious magic works with the deities and spirit beings closely associated with its practices, creating a spiritual and pyschic community within which (hopefully) things will happen according to the beliefs, prayers, and practices of the human participants.

In the standard religious model, the wishes of the spiritual allies are often neglected through emphasis upon prayer and ritual focusing on the needs of the supplicants, whereas in the folkloric magical models, the spiritual allies are given considerable respect, and their wishes explored and attended to. The first tends to be an action of repeated supplication, while the second tends to be an action of repeated mutual exchange.

In well-established folkloric magic, such as that of the many African traditions, there is a sophisticated technical knowledge, primarily concerned with ancestors and spirits within the sub-lunar realm. This type of magic can be very effective short-term, and is often frowned upon by westerners or esoteric students, who consider it "low" magic. As indeed it is from a metaphysical perspective, for it works directly within the lowest resonance or octave of consciousness/energy between moon and earth, impinging closely upon the human psyche and body. It is ethical intent that defines the quality of spiritual or magical endeavor, not any external value judgment. The occupants of the lower dimensions of the spiritual world, usually termed psychic planes, serve a powerful function when they are part of an organic hierarchy of spiritual transmission. When they are loose and chaotic, however, they can be misleading and dangerous, and may be coerced or bargained into unethical actions.

In religious magic, the rituals, prayers, contacts and so forth aim to bring in "higher" powers. Religious magic occurs when rituals are connected to a religion, be it eastern, western, or any other. Typically, the higher powers are those of a solar nature; the redeemers, saviors, certain but not all saints, and angelic or archangelic presences. Where gods and goddesses are involved, they are associated with solar and planetary forces and cosmic attributes. Some of the saints (inner contacts) are derived from folkloric magic, and from an esoteric perspective, these older forms are essential to link into the forces of the sub-lunar realm. The adaptation of older figures and images into a new religion (as has occurred in Christianity, Tibetan Buddhism and so forth) is really an organic alignment with the sub-lunar realm, political implications notwithstanding. The aim of religious magic is to draw the "higher" powers into the sub-lunar realm, and make changes according to tradition or according to the perceived need of the ritualists. We are all familiar with the terrible irony of two nations, each praying for victory over the other, each claiming to be righteous, each praying the the same "god". This is the inverse of righteousness, of course, the demonic warping of compassion into a selective selfish prayer: compassion for our side, destruction for theirs.

The Dream of the Sub-lunar Realm

The popular equation of the sub-lunar realm with the unconscious mind, the dream life, is pernicious. At its worst, it feeds into the humanocentric notion that all things exist only within the individual psyche, leading to that well known contemporary and virulent pseudo-spiritual narcissism, expressed as "I create my own reality". We do indeed create our own reality, usually from blunders, but only in, through, and as a result of, our interaction with the complex life forces within which we live, move, and have our being. If we seek, as the magician does, to re-shape that "reality" intentionally, we must first understand how our shaping is modulated by those complex life forces. Then we must discover how to *consciously participate* in the field within which we exist: in the perennial philosophy, metaphysics, and psychology, there is no unconscious or subconscious mind, there is only refusal to participate. Magical arts, meditation, contemplation visualization, higher forms of prayer, all gradually change our awareness, bringing it into a greater consciousness, a higher mode of participation.

Our first step towards participation is to discover where we live: our ground is primarily, on planet Earth, the sub-lunar realm. This realm is *plastic*, in the old fashioned meaning, adapted by science to substances made from petro-chemicals, and now having a range of contemporary meaning, but originally describing something malleable that will hold form after it has been shaped. These words are typed on an inert plastic keyboard, but the plasticity of the sub-lunar realm is a living field of energy, that may be molded by many, often seemingly contradictory, forces.

As mentioned above, we cannot truly participate in what are commonly called higher worlds until we have learned how to fully participate in this world. Such participation is a spiritual process, not a materialistic one. While it might be thought that we are referring to subtle propaganda of integration and adjustment in society, or to a stable daily life, these are merely story fragments that come and go. It is the subtle transformation through the spiritual forces of the planet that are our true reason for being here, and no storehouse of worldly acumen, no synthetic integration into a culture that is, by its nature, destructive to the human spirit, will substitute for such transformation. The late Dr. Arthur Guirdham (senior medical officer for the Bath area in Somerset, and well known author on the theme of reincarnation) once commented that he saw little point in prescribing psychiatric treatment or therapy for individuals when no attempt was made to heal or improve the society to which they were returned.

Once we have discovered, and experienced the effects of the UnderWorld, the faery realm at the Crossroads, the ancestral streams, the titanic planetary consciousnesses, we will have growing discernment and conscious participation. The Sphere of Art and the Two Sensitive Points will then enable us to move to another octave of participation, another cycle of energy and consciousness.

Chapter Three
Ethics and the Sphere of Art, Energies and Movements

The Problem of "Results"

There are many dynamic effects and results that arise from the Sphere of Art, and we will explore some of these shortly. Before we do so, we must reassess our modern attitude towards those "results" that we expect or demand. One of the questions that repeatedly comes up in classes and workshops is "what can I do with this?" This simple and not unreasonable question has been in the human consciousness since we picked up our first stick and explored its possibilities. But when you picked up that stick, you were concerned not merely with the potential for poking the fire or defense, but with the essential relationship between yourself and the stick...the you-ness and the stick-ness. This aspect has vanished from modern thought, as humanity has become increasingly detached from the surrounding and embracing world, and has moved into a state of isolation and antagonism. In brief "what can I do *with* this stick?" has become "how can I *use* this stick?", and from that moment our world of pollution, antagonism, and denial arises.

When the question is asked today it has modulated into a modern situational trap, whereby we are driven to deliver what appear to be results from any task. This trap arises from an educational model and a mind-set, with many variations, that broadly works as follows:

1 Develop some machine, tool, skill, and/or qualification to use same.

2 Do something with it.

3 Expect and deliver results promptly.

There would nothing inherently wrong with this mind-set, if it were founded upon a spiritual resource, and the progression from 1-3 above aimed to bring spiritual truth into manifestation: science and industry in compassionate service of humanity, rather than rabid with greed and indifferent to ethics, would be an excellent example of such a process. Indeed, the three steps described above are nothing less than a human attempt at mediating the forces of the Tree of Life. They have been the method of the practical magician for centuries, and we can detect this process in sources from Plato to the Renaissance and the Rosicrucians. By the time it manifests in 19th century occultism, however, it has lost much of its philosophical metaphysical foundation and become significantly mechanistic. In an attempt to move away from the problem of mere mechanism, which they clearly understood but could not resolve, early 20th century occultists enthusiastically proposed psychology as a solution. Yet thinkers and seers such as Rudolph Steiner perceived and declared, early on in this process, that psychology provided few solutions for the spiritual life, as it is little more than a thinly-veiled development of ultra-materialism[1].

At around the same time as Steiner, and in similar cultural circles in Europe, the philosopher Edmund Husserl (1859-1938) framed the *phenomenological* approach to philosophical exploration, which influenced modern writers such as Jean Paul Sartre (who later broke away from Husserl's theories). One of Husserl's fundamental assertions is startlingly similar to the methods of our Sphere of Art: *"Husserl's task is to get … into another "field"… It will be the sphere of absolute consciousness, consciousness when it isn't going anywhere… this will be "The Region of Pure Consciousness." You can't "go there" with consciousness; instead you have to let the worldly go away and then inhabit what's left. This is the import of the infamous fantasy that opens (Husserl's) paragraph 33: "(W)as kann als Sein noch setzbar sein, wenn das Weltall, das All der Realitat eingeklammert bleibt?" (In Kersten's paraphrase: "What can remain, if the whole world, including ourselves with all our cogitare, is excluded?"* [21]

I am not suggesting however, that Husserl's work was Qabalistic or esoteric, though it seems to share many themes with esoteric tradition, as does that of Sartre, and of Baudrillard[16] cited earlier, though both would laugh at this proposal. When the human intellect approaches questions of consciousness and perception, certain insights are bound to arise, regardless of the model or framework employed to describe such insights.

The contemporary mind is far, indeed, from either Steiner's spiritual psychology or Husserl's exclusion of cogitation, for it is obsessively result-driven. We see this in the shocking flaws of the education system, which places emphasis upon passing contrived tests, rather than upon actual learning or developing understanding. The result-obsessed consciousness is deeply ingrained in the global capitalist system, forming (as has long been observed) a powerful set of shackles for the individual who cannot see that he or she is merely a result-slave for the benefit of a minority that holds authority and power. Nor should we see this trap as being uniquely modern: in the historical Christian world of previous centuries, result-driven indoctrination revolved around sin and salvation, and is, to this day, the source of our contemporary trap in many ways. If you can get results, you are good…if not…well, you are just a bad inefficient individual and will sink to the bottom of the heap. You no longer go to hell, because like Mephistopheles in Marlowe's Faustus, you are already there.

Earlier we discussed the problem of simulation, replacing our relationship with the natural world. Such simulation is widespread in internet fantasy, even to the extend of simulated "worlds" in which members earn simulated money, and acquire simulated wealth and property. Such fantasy is also result-driven, whereby the simulation of a result within a computer program is regarded as some kind of desirable end.

When we work with the Sphere of Art and the Two Sensitive Points, we have to let go of the contemporary illusion of results. Only by doing so will we discover the potential results that will arise from the energies in the Sphere. This is perhaps frustrating for the modern mind, a situation of axiological ethics rather than obvious practicalities.

Ethics Make Things Work

From time to time we find remarkable individuals who devise equipment and theories that seem to by-pass the generally accepted laws of physics. In our Introduction, we cited the work of Luis Rota as a powerful example. Yet problems arise when their theories and practical examples are attempted by others…for they only work for the originator. Contemporary science solves this paradox by declaring the source to be fraudulent, end of story. Yet advanced modern physics repeatedly asserts that the scientist and the experiment interact, and that consciousness and expectations will affect the outcome of any process. Such understanding is not new, and is the basis of all magical arts, metaphysics, and spiritual disciplines. When remarkable results cannot be duplicated according to the basic disciplines of materialist science, this may be due to the consciousness and expectations of the operatives, and not necessarily due to the theory experiment or equipment, all of which may have worked well for its originator.

This situation is one of ethics rather than of nuts and bolts. The state of consciousness, the ethical nature, the spiritual condition, are all major factors in the subtle forces behind our manifest elements and energies. Before we can understand what we may "do" with the Sphere of Art, we must first begin to understand this matter of ethics: after this initial effort, it is our work with the Sphere itself that brings us into a condition of ethical transformation. Unless we move some way towards this, we will not be able to achieve certain results through the Sphere, just as certain alchemical and energetic experiments and actions cannot be infinitely repeated by anyone who only has the basic method described in a text, but does not have the consciousness required to make it work.

More simply we can answer the perennial question "what can I do with this" by saying "first discover what this will do with you". The key concept is *with*, not in the sense of using, but in the sense of mutual interaction. That first stick, held in your hand long ago deep in ancestral time, was used to draw a circle in the sand. From that moment on, you were a magician exploring the cosmos consciously, and discovering how to interact with the cosmos consciously. The Sphere of Art is the next stage. The Sphere brings us into a conscious interaction with the cosmos through exclusion of the sub-lunar realm. That is all that we do with the Sphere, and the rest is helpful commentary or elucidation.

The First Ethical Step: Relating to the Sub-lunar Realm

Before going further, it should be stated that this is not going to be an exposition on morals, diet, substance abuse, laziness or sexuality. These are petty details that we all have to work with, in our own lives, on our own responsibility. If we cannot clear up these basics, which are repeatedly blown out of all proportion in our culture (probably to keep us focused upon them at all costs), we might as well continue to passively watch television or play internet games. Working with the Sphere will help you with inner weaknesses and imbalances, providing you really wish to adjust them, but much of the ground work (in the sub-lunar realm) has to be done by you, in its natural state, day by day. In other words, we have to follow through.

The first ethical step, therefore, is to understand *not* why we might seek to exclude the forces of the sub-lunar world, but why these forces are sacred, even in exclusion. There must be no value judgment in clearing and stilling the Sphere, no trace of rejection, reaction, emotional gratification, in our exclusion of the sub-lunar world. Indeed, what we are doing is a simple action similar to tidying a room, putting certain things in certain places, and making a clear space for what will happen next. This action of tidying or clearing is immensely powerful.

Our first ethical step (of three) is fruitful in both contemplation and in action. While developing our exclusion of the subtle forces of the sub-lunar realm, we might consider the question: "where do they go?"

When the sub-lunar forces are outside the Sphere, they align upon its boundary, and provide an external polarized energy for its field or shield. Far from "banishing" them, we are aligning them into their primary purpose, which is to work as a skin or membrane between the stellar or originative spiritual powers and the manifest world. When this membrane receives imprints, it holds them and re-iterates them, sometimes briefly, sometimes for millenniums. By working with the Sphere of Art, we are able to propose, to initiate, *imprints from within the Sphere* to the assembled sub-lunar forces that are, so to speak, glued to its surface. The imprints will permeate this glue of forces, and modify them. They are then picked up by the lunar tides, and circulated. This is a different proposition to the dreary old standard of will-power in magic, or to the traditional methods of working with spirit allies and making pacts in order to modify the sub-lunar patterns, as discussed in Chapter Two.

The Second Ethical Step: Becoming Void

After coming into a state of purified relationship with the sub-lunar forces that are exterior, we must next define and clarify our relationship to the spiritual forces within the Sphere of Art. The basic method, as stated above, requires Stillness: emptying the Sphere. What about our relationship to that Emptiness? We must also be still, and become void, within ourselves. This is a slow and ongoing process, whereby any ulterior motive or attachment to the power of the Sphere is unraveled steadily and persistently. Here is where the popular delusion of "will power" arises, one of the most misleading concepts found in magical and spiritual literature. We need strength of will to persist in any task, but it must be applied to ends that are ultimately non-personal. If the will is repeatedly associated with the personality we cannot be void and still, as the personality is ceaselessly searching for ways to reinforce itself through will. Only when we open out this loop, releasing and recycling the enormous energy tied into it, can we transform.

While the glue that adheres subtle sub-lunar patterns to the exterior of the Sphere is the foundation of manifest form, the will is that which can modify this foundation prior to its manifestation. In a habitual life, lived mostly in an unconscious manner, the will personality and foundational forces interact in a reactive mode most of the time, rather like the seemingly random swimming of a shoal of fish. Only by observing that shoal from a distance can we sense its patterns, but when we are within it we are just swimming from point to point in order to survive day by day. A natal chart is a good example of such observation from a distance, though there are many others.

In our analogy it might seem absurd for the individual fish to seek to control the shoal, and if that fish exerts its will to go counter to the mass, it loses its congruity with the greater collective, and will usually fail to thrive. Yet humans frequently seek to control their collective, and through inflated will can rise, albeit briefly, to positions of worldly power. These do not last long.

While the first ethical position was to understand that the sublunar forces are sacred, the second is to remove the personality from within the Sphere of Art: only when there is no personal agenda or self-interest will the transformative power of the Sphere of Art and the Two Sensitive Points work at maximum. To a certain extent we must acknowledge that this is an on-going process, and that there is no specific arrival point at which we might say "now I have done it". Moving deeply into the state on un-being, of the void, is not a matter of abstract contemplation or withdrawal, as is often assumed and taught. It is an ethical position of consciousness, that has potent effects on the sub-lunar world and thereby changes the manifest world. As the personality is typically a loosely woven accident, tossed around lifetime after lifetime until it is knocked into shape, it must be regarded as a temporary vehicle rather than a permanent situation. Exceptions to this are what we might call custom or sculpted personalities taken on as masks by evolved souls, who come into incarnation with specific tasks to fulfill. In such cases, the mask is often molded through the conception and birth patterns shown in the natal chart.

Yet, you will say, is it not true that most spiritual teachers or leaders have strong personalities? The answer to this question depends on the type of personality exhibited by the teacher: is it dramatic and flamboyant, or is it truly out of the ordinary and impossible to measure by cultural standards? The first is an interim stage that we all go through as our consciousness expands and develops, while the second is a result of going further into the void, the source of that expanded consciousness. Some spiritual mediators are singularly bland and unnoticeable…this applies to both the ethical and the corrupt.

Within the Sphere, the most important form is that of Stillness. Stilling our interaction with Time, Space, and Movement becomes more than a meditative process, and opens out as a source of what can seem, in heightened moments, to be illimitable power. But if this power is entrapped by the personality, both the power and the personality can become warped. The illimitable power referred to is not personal, but universal. We can participate in it, but never own it. The analogy to the swimmer or surfer riding the ocean waves holds good: if we ride them and flow with them, they support and move us, if we seek to control or fight them, we are lost. This absence of personal investment in power is why the adept rarely projects gold from lead. True gold is a spiritual process, not a psychological or physical integration or illumination. Any spiritual process is capable of direct manifestation, if we could but know the paths appropriate to it: the Sphere of Art is one such path.

The Third Ethical Step: Aligning to Spiritual Impetus

The sub-lunar forces have been excluded, but not rejected. They have their task to fulfill. Within the Sphere we also have our task to fulfill, which cannot be undertaken until we are empty and still. The third ethical step is one of *alignment*.

To what do we align, from our place of stillness? This is another of those significant choices whereby the work is sacromagical, rather than isolated, introverted, or contemplative. For, in this art, we place our potential, our void, in service of a spiritual impetus.

This spiritual impetus comes from inner or metaphysical dimensions, and seeks to directly accelerate the transformative forces that work upon our manifest world. There is no "message" or religious teaching, and no formal organization. The impulse is organic, in the sense that it works through the laws of life that form the fabric of the cosmos, which are mirrored in our manifest world. Yet there are intelligences that draw close to us, through the mediating vessel of the Sphere, and which can commune with us through the Two Sensitive Points.

The sensitive points are more than a Shortened Way of initiation for us: they are a short-cut through time and space whereby we come into communion with higher forms of consciousness. Such beings are timeless, in that they are trans-lunar, and not bound by the cycles of the Wheel of Fortune. Yet, to we who are bound by time, they may reveal the potential future: not as events, but as a new mode of consciousness, a new way of being[19]. This is the true uplifting of the world into spiritual grace…not an escape or a dualistic rejection, but a total transformation that is all inclusive. None are left behind, none are damned.

The level of spiritual contact within the Sphere is direct, rather than conversational or intellectual. By coming into this communion we receive it and carry it in our bodies, not in our minds as words or teachings. When we say *in our bodies*, this must mean all aspects of our being, from the spiritual through the mental and emotional, into the physical. When the mental and emotional bodies are made still and void, the spiritual passes directly into the physical. From the physical the spiritual communion and power arises into the mental and emotional bodies that are still and void, filling, clarifying, and energizing them.

The Lightning Flash

A circuit is created, therefore, within the individual, which is an octave or resonance of the circuit within the Sphere. This enables a Lightning Flash to spark between the Two Sensitive Points. It must be understood that the Sphere would not work without the human component, and the human component would not transform rapidly without the Sphere. Nor should we presume that the human contribution is the only one of value or power, for the interactions in the Sphere are a fourfold combination of human, transhuman, archangelic, and cosmic forces. These have a broad relationship to the Four Elements and Directions as follows:

Human: Water/Love/West
Transhuman: Air/Life /East
Archangelic: Fire/Light /South
Cosmic: Earth/Law/North

If we meditate upon these contributing spiritual powers, we should approach them in the following order:

1 Cosmic Earth Law
2 Archangelic Fire Light
3 Transhuman Air Life
4 Human Water Love

A pattern that moves North/South/East/West.

Thus the Cosmic Earth Law forces are the highest, permeating the universe, mirrored by the laws of energy within the telluric fire of our planet. What we normally think of as laws are the most manifest part of the spectrum of cosmic law. This is why the Grail, vessel of Grace and Regeneration, is a hidden Stone within the earth.

We must also remember that the Elements are never rigid, but are constantly interacting with one another[20]. As an example, there is no "pure fire", but there is creative and destructive energy that partakes more of fire than of any other element, and has relatively little of the other three within it. This relative pattern is the key to understanding the four elements of the cosmos.

The power that sparks in our ceremony is that which transforms lead into gold…known only in the underworld of deep earth shielded from lunar influence, and recreated in the Sphere of Art. This shielding from Lunar influence is paradoxical, for the lunar womb is essential to the birth, providing its subtle flux does not touch the interior and content of the vessel, providing that it remains as a field or shield around the circumference.

The New Sun

Under certain conditions, a *new sun* is born in the center of the Sphere. If we are able to receive this new sun into ourselves we can carry it to the outer world of nature through the simple act of walking on the surface of the earth. By further practices we are able to walk the power of the new sun into the body of the planet, where it will work its alchemical magic.[18]

The birth of the new sun is an act of fusion, not of fission. The stellar fire entering through the sensitive point above, fuses with the telluric fire entering through the sensitive point below. To explore how we may relate further, we return to our discussion of the Zones of the Body:

Zones of the Body in the Sphere of Art

The zones of the body that are activated through the Sphere of Art are as follows:
1 The brow, head, and above the head: Stellar
2 The heart and lungs: Solar
3 The loins and genitals: Lunar
4 The feet and below the feet: Earth

In habitual living, when the consciousness does not participate in the four relationships shown above, but tends to be driven
willy nilly by distraction and countless influences, these zones are
typically disconnected from one another in a variety of ways. This
"disconnection" is neither rigid nor permanent, but changeable and
slippery, though tending towards fixity as we grow older. It becomes
especially fixed through reinforcement by addictive patterns of con-
sumption, behavior, and imagination, unhealthy imagination being
the most powerful fixative. Just as the imagination can rigidify dis-
connections of the subtle flow between the four zones, so is it the
cure. If we purify our imaginations, all else will follow[9]. Relationship and interaction between the four zones will change through our
lives, depending on experience, natural forces of growth or limita-
tion, and on any spiritual practices that we undertake.

Variations of this teaching are found in many traditions, as it
reports human experience, so will be found often with cultural and
religious modifications. Our aim here is twofold: to make it as clear
and simple as possible without unusual vocabulary, and to clarify
it for intense practical use within the Sphere. Before you read this
section, you should read again the caution regarding contemporary
"chakra" practices in Chapter One, as this model is not based on the
popular chakra systems in general publication.

Within our context of the Sphere of Art, we can focus on forms
and methods that accelerate interaction between the zones of the
body and the cosmos. This is done without invocation, without deities, and, most especially, without focusing on the zones themselves.
If you focus repeatedly on the zones attempting to stimulate them
by concentration or breathing, you will only reinforce any isolation
or disharmony within you. Such direct focusing, highly emphasized
in modern chakra practices, is similar to the popular idea of body
building and using steroids. The result can be a superficially impres-
sive overdeveloped musculature, which has no graceful function,
and cannot do anything other than seek to maintain its un-natural
condition. Chakra-dogma practices are similar to pumping iron…
they can only perpetuate themselves and have no further function.

Within the Sphere, through not focusing upon the zones or
seeking to develop them, we *allow* the zones to come more fully

alive, and to move into harmony with one another. This condition is opened only by becoming empty, opening within ourselves the first principle of Being, which is the Void.

While becoming empty and void is typically described as a meditative or contemplative practice, here it is a *ritual form*, under highly energized conditions created within the Sphere.

A classic Qabalistic teaching refers to the head as being an entire Tree of Life, as is the body. We can extend this to the Zones: each of the zones listed above is entire Tree of Life, with that below the feet comprising our roots, our connection to the UnderWorld planetary tree. This should not create yet more pointless check-lists, as in 19th century occultism, but gradually it may become an intimation *felt within the body*. This is the basis for meditations upon the internal organs, referred to by various writers including Rudolph Steiner, whose work is substantially based upon Qabalah. By meditation upon the internal organs, our forebears did not mean something grisly or fleshy, but the zones or vessels within which our manifest organs are contained and protected. Furthermore, most internal meditation tends to be abstract, often seeking to work with fantastical and eminently inapplicable notions of energy flow and chakras. We can greatly improve our subtle energies by communicating with our internal organs, which are usually ignored until they break down. By this simple action alone, we stimulate subtle energies, without focusing on the energies themselves.

1 The Stellar zone of above the head, brow (face), and neck vertebrae is a stellar Tree of Life, mirroring the three supernal spheres of Crown, Wisdom, and Understanding. This is the Hallowing Vessel, that Hallows the Sacred Name of Being.

2 The Solar zone of heart and lungs (chest, arms, and hands) is a solar Tree of Life, mirroring the spheres of Beauty, Mercy, and Severity. This is the Justified Vessel that balances forgiveness and rigor, creation and destruction, through a central organ of harmony.

3 The Lunar zone of loins and genitals (organs in the lower body) is a lunar Tree of Life, mirroring the spheres of Foundation, Glory, and Power. This is the Enabling Vessel that enables birth and death, motion into and out of manifestation.

4 The Earth zone mirrors the inverted tree, the UnderWorld Tree of Life, and its kingdom and crown is in the soles of our feet.

This is not, as we might expect, the manifest vessel, but the Hidden Vessel. This vessel connects us to the Grail within the Earth, the UnderWorld of regeneration. The Manifest Vessel, The Kingdom, is our entire body, within the holism of the manifest cosmos.

Each of the four zones has within it certain key components which have practices associated with them. The two most important are 1 and 4 listed above.

1 The first zone includes brow and above the head, but also extends through the entire head to the neck. In the human body we might expect the link to the sensitive point above to be above the head: but is in the neck, where the neck joins the spine, just above the shoulders. From this point in the back of the neck, the spirit cord[9] extends upwards to the sensitive point above.

4 The fourth zone includes the feet and below the feet. From the soles of the feet the spirit cord extends into the Earth Light, the UnderWorld, through the sensitive point below.

As discussed, these forms are modular: they must be practiced in sequence, as described. After some skill has been developed, the forms are then combined. With repeated practice the modular forms flow into one another, and can be opened out rapidly.

The Transcendent Linear Movements

At this point in the exposition, we can explore the significance of the relationships between the directions as two linear movements: East-West, and North-South.

This theme of *direction* and movement is central to all magical arts, as it is rooted in the essential nature of the cosmos, and its movement from the Void to Manifestation, from Manifestation to the Void. If we truly knew *how to move* we would have knowledge of the cosmos…but the mind alone cannot hold such knowledge, for it is of a higher order than our mental processes. We can, however, mirror certain aspects of the movement of the cosmos in our sacromagical work: this much is well known in tradition. Surprisingly little attention has been paid to the selection and definition of specific movements in ritual and to their effects. While there is ample literature and media on dance forms and martial arts, most of it takes a popular form, often relating to a "feel-good" factor or to

fitness development, or both. Sacromagical movement is not limited
to ritual dance, nor is it solely martial arts, though both are derived
from such cosmic sacromagical movement, even in their most crude
or popular presentations.

Typically modern magical arts focus on the circular or spiral
movement of the directions: E/S/W/N. This concept is widely found
in all forms of contemporary magic, from pagan and witchcraft rituals to Hermetic lodge ceremonies. It is also, of course, embedded in
tradition in many forms, and found throughout the world, from the
directions of the Hindu Temple to the alignments of the megalithic
standing stones of Britain, Ireland, and western Europe. This movement of E/S/W/N is a reiteration of the cycle of the day, the seasons
of the year, the phases of life, and is well known to anyone familiar
with modern and traditional magic. It also appears, as an implicit
pattern, in many aspects of folkloric magic, from faery tradition to
communal ceremonies handed down through the generations, and a
deeper understanding of folkloric magic can be opened by exploring
it in the context of the Four Directions.

We might easily think that the "implicit" or sub-conscious presence of the cycle of the directions may be due to degeneration of
tradition or loss of explication, but there is another, more significant, reason. Until recently, people lived with a greater awareness of
the sky, the seasons, the passage of moon, sun, and stars. Only with
the growth of urbanism and modernism have we lost that awareness, though it still remains inherent within our bodies and our
consciousness. While much of modern revival magic concerns itself
with re-attuning to the directions, the seasons, the planetary forces,
most ancestral magic took these truths of life on Earth for granted,
and employed them as a foundation and starting point for further
movement. Thus modern magic, paganism, and witchcraft must,
quite appropriately, return to the basics that were inherent in the
consciousness of our ancestors. There is no need, however, for us to
remain with those basics as our sole field of endeavor, once we have
re-established them, and re-connected to that deep ancestral perception of the directions, moon, sun, stars, and seasons.

Contemporary magical ceremonies seek, appropriately, to re-
awaken that sense of relationship to the seasonal cycle that is shown

in the E/S/W/N pattern, and to the inherent elemental cycle of manifestation and change. This cycle is the Wheel, be it the Wheel of Fortune in western, or the wheel of karma in eastern traditions. Ceremony and ritual in general tend to work within the cycle of the Wheel, which is a *sub-lunar* cycle of Fortune, mirroring the powers of Justice, the greater wheel of the Solar System. The ultimate wheel is that of Judgment, the enfolding sphere of space time and stars, as shown in our Figure Four.

There are, however, a number of other movements within the circle/sphere that have special significance. The Lightning Flash or "Z" movement is one found in both western and eastern esoteric traditions, and has been discussed elsewhere[13, 15]. We will return to some hitherto unpublished aspects of the Lightning Flash in volume two, but first we must explore the most simple and yet profound movements, those between the poles of east and west, and north and south. *The following examples should be practiced within the activated Sphere of Art.*

The East-West and North-South Extensions

A line (or movement) is an extension of a point: from stillness to movement. By extension we both define A and B, where only a hitherto undefined point (pre-A) existed, and we connect A and B through movement in space and time. This is the truth and paradox of the creation of the cosmos. The Sphere of Art mirrors the cosmos, and is a vessel within which the cosmic processes are generated afresh. This same modeling or mirroring is found in the use of the vessel in alchemy, and is of the womb-nature of the cosmos.

East-West

From a human perspective, when we move on the circular flat plain or ground within the defined and energized sphere, the east-west line or extension is the movement of each incarnation and birth, and each excarnation and death: it is, in essence, the movement of the Soul. Such movement is mirrored incessantly in our emotions and our vital forces from birth to death: from Life to Love.

North-South

The north-south line or extension is the movement of consciousness beyond and between incarnations, of the source or origin of the soul, the movement of spirit: this movement is mirrored in our higher awareness, and in our bodies, from Law to Light. It can be discovered in the death of the body in the North and its return to a cosmic awareness in the South, a movement that we have all experienced many times prior to engagement with the Wheel and rebirth.

Both movements, east-west and north-south, are consubstantial and concinnate: present in the twin streams of red and white, blood and water/seed, the Red and White Dragons of bardic tradition, which embody the evolutionary and involutionary streams radiating off- and on-planet. Yet in our manifest lives we tend always towards blood as the east-west movement, and water/seed as the north-south movement. We will return to this abstruse but not unapproachable idea again, for it is the *turning about* of this tendency that brings higher consciousness, transforming the flow of blood/water and changing their direction. Many hints and perplexing descriptions of this process are found in magical and metaphysical texts from various traditions. The Sphere of Art enables it to happen, in a direct manner.

The Hidden Rivers

There are also movements of subtle energy west-east, and south-north. The Hidden Rivers of the world flow counter to the manifest rivers: from the ocean to the land, in the west-east movement. This invisible but tangible counter-movement can be tapped in our magical work. The hidden river that flows west-east provides a vast source of power for magical work[15].

Likewise the south-north movement is the power of the ubiquitous earth-light, which comprises one of the rivers of the Under-World, so strongly described in both classical Greek and northern European faery tradition.

These seemingly cryptic statements can be opened out into application in practical work, both as physical movements of the body (or group) and in individual work in empowered vision, meditation, and contemplation. The subtle forces of the sacromagical sphere will move in such patterns spontaneously, with our participation, and even without it, and we may work with this movement.

The East-West Linear Movement

There are three stages to each of the linear movements: point of origin, still point at the center, and point of conclusion. The principle of *extension* both links and defines them...they are in potential before extension, and in relationship after extension. With this concept we are reminded of the function of the four magical implements, Sword, Rod, Cup, and Shield. Each of these embodies, in the manifest world of substance, a mode of *extension* and *reception* of extension. This comprises a powerful meditation that brings many insights.

Note: for the descriptions which follow you will find that drawing the patterns is helpful as a first stage, then stepping through them in the manner of rehearsal without activating the Sphere. Only when you have practiced the forms, and meditated on their action, should you activate the Sphere and go into them in greater depth.

Any linear movement or extension that we make with our bodies in the Sphere will initiate deeper understanding of the cycles of Birth-Death-Rebirth: in effect linear extension can, if worked correctly, transcend and transform the typical cycle of the Wheel. Movements cycling E/S/W/N are sun-wise (often unfortunately called "clockwise"), while movements N/W/S/E are star-wise. Once again, this much was obvious in the diurnal and nocturnal lives of our ancestors, but has been lost to modern people.

Within the three-stage movement described above, from east to center to west, we can discern, relate to, and activate other subtle stages.

First stage to second stage: Commencing in the East, the first stage of the linear movement gathers energy from the cycles E/S and E/N simultaneously. Spirit moves from Life to Light, and from Life to Law, two polar currents of energy working together: the E/S is part of the familiar sun-wise cycle E/S/W/N, while the E/N is part of the star-wise cycle E/N/W/S. In human terms, by moving through the still point of the centre, from East towards West, we are moving simultaneously from birth to death E/N, and birth to adulthood E/S, with one direct movement, pausing at then passing through a point of stillness in the Centre. By this movement, we extend and *fuse* our evolutionary and involutionary processes as one. In contrast to this spiritual movement, our normal death process is one of fission, in which things break apart, be it a pattern within any life-cycle, or the death of the body.

Second stage to third stage: From the still point of the Center, we move towards the West. This movement partakes of the cycles S/W (sun-wise) and N/W (star-wise), Light to Love, Law to Love. In human terms this is a simultaneous passage from peak adulthood to maturity and through death to maturity of consciousness. This gives us some insights into the traditional associations of the west with death and the otherworld.

Observe that each stage of the East-West movement has within its star-wise segments long term implications, for E/N is birth to death...an entire lifetime. This entire lifetime of E/N star-wise is extended *in reverse* to our normal perceptions, which tend to attune E/S/W/N, or birth adulthood maturity, death, around the Wheel. N/W is death to maturity, the initiatory cycle or Shortened Way towards a maturity of spirit, a developed consciousness that is not limited by manifestation in Nature.

Thus far, we have emphasized a human linear extension as physical movement, crossing the mid-plane of the Sphere of Art (the floor of the Circle), through the center. This simple movement has profound implications, and substantial transformative effects, *providing we participate in it consciously.*

The basic rule for all sacromagical movements is that we must know how to make the movement, identify why we are making it, and begin to discern those deeper forces inherent within the movement: forces that may come into our consciousness/energy and initiate transformation. At the deepest levels of spiritual magic we work with *intention* and *participation* rather than mental interpretation. The linear movements and extensions are not symbolic, but participatory. Never think of them as symbols or diagrams...this is the most superficial level, beyond which many students never reach. Symbols and diagrams are maps, helpful indeed, but they are not the journey itself.

The North-South Linear Movement

This extension is from Law to Light, and its first stage (moving towards the centre) is simultaneous with the cycles N/E and N/W…Law to Life, and Law to Love. The N/E cycle is our movement between manifest lives, between death and rebirth. It transits that significant point of the north-east, the Janus threshold between the inner dimensions and the outer world of nature. The N/W cycle is a star-wise movement, from death and the spiritual dimensions, towards maturity in manifestation. It also the Shortened Way or initiatory path of the Hanged Man…who is suspended from the Tree atop the mountain of the North, with his head in the waters flowing below, the West.[22] In this context we might also meditate on the star-wise movements in relationship to supernal trump images: Hanged Man, Temperance, The Star, and Judgement.

Following our linear extension, north to south, we move from the still point of the centre, to the south. This is simultaneous with the cycles E/S (sun-wise), and W/S (star-wise). East-South is the increase of Illumination, and west-south is found in the image of Fire over Water. *Fire Over Water* is a key image of the Atlantean Fire Temple, and is found repeatedly in Dion Fortune's novel the *Sea Priestess* as the ritual of fire at the shoreline. Originally the image was that of a volcano arising out of the ocean. Later this image becomes that of the Pyramid.

These hints are intended to be subjects for meditation, which can be done under almost any circumstances. After meditation on the extensions and movements, they should be practiced, one by one, within the activated Sphere of Art.

Conclusion

By now you will have discovered that the practices described may not be undertaken lightly or superficially: there are responsibilities to accept, and you have to focus and be disciplined. Beyond this early training stage of discipline and responsibility, the methods become simple and clear, opening within us a regenerated awareness that perceives that the world of nature, the sub-lunar world, is already one with the cosmos. In old fashioned language, these practices return us to a fully conscious state, into the condition before "the Fall" from cosmic awareness towards increasing isolation. This is not an intellectual or philosophical concept, but a radically altered awareness. It can be described in words, but it can only be experienced through itself.

One of the classic paradoxes in human life is the task of reconciling the spiritual, the numinous, the inspirational, with the grisly task of day to day existence. In our modernist culture (formerly and inaccurately described as "western", but now permeating the planet) a lucrative luxury industry has arisen purporting to help us reconcile these contradictory modes of life. The emphasis of this industry is upon self-development and self-gratification. In the deeper spiritual traditions, however, the emphasis is upon service and compassion, bearing in mind that such radiant concepts have been greatly abused and propagandized by orthodox religions. We come into this world not to scrabble for its material or personal benefits and then die, but to serve the long term task of transformation and evolution of consciousness. Not for our ephemeral personalities, but for a greater consciousness of which we are a part. Thus the individual life be-comes less significant, less of an ego-drama, while growing more intense, vibrant, and increasingly aware and alive.

For many people on this planet, the task of living is one of bare survival in appalling hostile circumstances. The popular fanfares of modernism, declaring that we live in a world where technology sets us free, and of New Age dogma, insisting that we live in a world of rapid personal growth and enlightenment, are both escapist delusions. Such fantasies, one overtly materialist, the other covertly so, can only be indulged in through an intentional rejection of compassion at the agonized expense of those millions less fortunate than ourselves.

When you meditate, when you join a ritual, remember first those who are not allowed to do so, either by circumstances or oppressive tyrannies of religion or politics. Only a very small number of people on the planet have the right to religious freedom and spiritual exploration, either in law or within cultural limits.

If we have the luxury of exploring the spiritual life, rather than having to fight for food, shelter, and safety, we have been given a responsibility. Our responsibility is to explore and open out those realms of consciousness that cannot be accessed by those less fortunate than ourselves. We do this not for ourselves alone, but for those who cannot yet do so for themselves. By acting thus, our efforts resonate out to many, through the homeopathic or catalyzing principle that a tiny energy will leaven and eventually transform the mass. Significantly, through accepting this responsibility we find our own liberation from the inhibiting cycles and patterns that arise in all lives, be they privileged or not. We are no longer indulging in the solipsistic solo lament of "why does it happen to me?", but joining instead the choir of subtle harmonies that steadily modifies planetary awareness.

Writing on the theme of prophecy in the early 1970's, A. R. Heaver stated: *"Inevitably the presentation of such a theme as this brings up the age-old controversy of predestination versus free will. But there is no real difficulty in reconciling these apparently contradictory principles once we see that both operate on separate yet complementary wave lengths"*.

One of the most pernicious and vicious New Age concepts that is often voiced and published is that unfortunate people in the Third World cultures have brought misery and conflict upon themselves by "creating their own reality". In an older, equally vicious paradigm, it would have been argued that they were predestined to their suffering, with the later added corollary that they are not yet evolved sufficiently to transform it. The idea of separate yet complementary wavelengths described above by ARH can bring us into a new level of understanding that disposes of both of these simplistic and divisive ideas.

The methods of the Sphere of Art and the Two Sensitive points are the beginning of a radical path of regeneration. While we are entitled to clarify our own awareness by any means possible upon the path of individual liberation from delusion and suppression, such a clarification has limitations. Such limitations are due, of course, to focussing solely upon "the self". Paradoxically, when we stop focusing upon the self and endeavor to seek liberation for many, the individual regenerative process leaps forward.

R. J. Stewart, California, 2008

Appendix One
Memoir of Meeting Ronald Heaver

This expanded article on Alfred Ronald Heaver (ARH), was first published in Avalon Magazine, Glastonbury, Britain, Spring 2006. An earlier (shorter) version was first published online in 2005, and this appears as a preface to the Inner Temple Traditions Inner Convocation meditations which can be found at http://www.rjstewart.org/inner-temples-5a.html.

Opening note: Some of this story and associated teachings have been shared with students at workshops and classes from 1989 to the present year, while many of the spiritual themes are found in my books and recordings.

The meetings described in this article happened in the mid- to late-1970's. By this time, many of the outward activities of ARH's life had gradually faded, and he was making ready for his conscious death, which he knew would occur on the 10th of February 1980, his 80th birthday.

Before recounting my meetings with ARH, I would like to share some brief insights regarding the teaching methods and general consciousness of the older generation of mentors in Britain. I am referring to those who, like ARH, had come through World War One and/or World War Two. Few of them are left now. Many people today do not understand how different their methods were from those familiar to us in the last 20 years of spiritual, pagan, and New Age revival. There is, as a result, romanticizing, even fantasizing, about some of the founders of our spiritual and magical revival, and especially that powerful branch that relates so strongly to Glastonbury and the Sacred Mysteries.

Later in this article I describe some of the remarkable un-teaching methods that I experienced from sitting with ARH ... in some ways he taught nothing, in other ways he taught everything, all at once, like a massive instantaneous download, that had to be decrypted and digested. Some of the inner spiritual material I received from him is still unfolding in me today, thirty years later. Indeed, I now understand that ARH, and the spiritual lineage that he embodied, set certain tasks for me that I am still fulfilling. Some of this work appears in my books, often in unlikely guise. It was ARH, for example, that planted the seeds that led my writing of *The Under-World Initiation* in the late 1970's. But most significantly, it was he who brought me into the work that later on became my Inner Temple Traditions Inner Convocation classes and groups, which are now found in many parts of the USA, Canada, Britain, and Europe.

The Spiritual Teaching Methods of the Wartime Generation

Some of the methods of that older wartime generation of spiritual mentors may seem strange to us, but were essential to them in their day. This background, both individual and cultural, is helpful to our understanding of ARH's life and work, as he was of that generation, though in many ways he rose above it, despite a most difficult and dramatic life.

Firstly, many of these older generation teachers, mentors, and mystics of the British inner tradition, be they known or unknown, would teach different, even contradictory things, to different students. Therefore, students learning individually from one teacher, would each receive variations or even contradictions of the core teachings. This method was widespread, and was not as frivolous as we might think. Another method, which was well known, though supposedly secret, was to give an initiation or a confirmation of spiritual power, then tell the recipient that only he or she had received it. Years later, the recipients (plural) would find others who had had the same experience! There are typically certainly key secret phrases and dramatic unique subtle sensations, so no one (but no one) can fake receiving such spiritual empowerments.

There was also an emphasis on strict authority, which sits uncomfortably with us today. However, when we think of the genuine masters, mentors and teachers associated with Glastonbury and the British Mysteries, from occultists and mystics such as Dion Fortune through to luminaries such as Tudor Pole and Ronald Heaver, their authority was deep and clean. They all had an undeniable presence. By comparison, anyone who demands or enforces respect (before they dole out "teachings") is not worthy of it, and has no true authority.

So what purpose did all this secrecy, bifurcation of teachings and authority serve? We might think that it came from the secretive mentality of 19th century occultism, developed in a repressed culture, and (of course) from the overall concern about religious persecution that has haunted mystics, pagans, and magicians throughout the Christian era. But there is more to it than this, and I propose, without going into detailed historical proof in this short article, that the same methods had been in use for many centuries, long predating the Christian era. We know, for example, that the Ancient Mysteries of the pagan classical world kept their lines of authority secret, and that initiates remained anonymous. This is but one fragment of the historical foundation of the secrecy that permeated 19th and early 20th century occultism and magic. One day someone will write a book on it, but it will not be me.

There are other reasons why such methods arose, and deeper enlightenment on such secrecy was given to me by W. G. Gray, another mentor of that same generation, who appears again later in this article. He taught that the inner traditions used a cell system for continuity…whereby only a small number of people knew one another directly, usually no more than four or five, no matter how large the overall lineage or stream might be. And no one knew everyone. This method, he affirmed, had been widely used in the secret magical groups and orders in Europe and Russia. This, he said, was to ensure survival. But there is more to this cell system than an underground continuity, for it has resonance with the planetary life itself.

Esoteric Transmission Modeled on the World of Nature

Nowadays we might see these methods of transmission not so much as political, but as something akin to organic growth…a consciousness, a spiritual flower or tree, if you wish, that extends many roots and branches, and then puts forth many seeds. The seeds do not know of one another, when the wind blows them, but they all partake, genetically of the same tree. In this case, the genetics are spiritual, rather than biological. Even if the original plant dies or is cut down, it continues through its offspring. This same protean growth through multiple strands, extends through all planetary life, down to the cellular level. This significant connection advises us that the older generation teachers were concerned more with long-term continuity, than with short term authority, organization, grades, or hierarchies; such petty things were, and still are, for the juveniles.

I have no doubt that the influence of ARH has been protean and organic in this manner, and that is precisely why there is no organization or outer hierarchy associated with him. Nor should there ever be, for that would be a grave backward step. Such an organization would be the opposite of all his deep intentions. Furthermore, his life was clearly a dramatic and inevitable movement away from organization and groups in his early years and middle life, towards a deeper spiritual mediation (mediation, not meditation) in his mature and most powerful years.

Finally, we need to remind ourselves that such mentors and exemplars as Ronald Heaver, Tudor Pole, George Trevelyan, and many more, had been through either one or two terrible wars, which had left indelible marks upon their individual psyches, often upon their bodies (as was the case with ARH), and upon the entire generations of which they were a part. We can only truly understand the exterior of their lives, personalities, and teachings in that context. The inner aspects, of course, are timeless.

Meeting Ronald Heaver in the 1970's.

In the mid-1970's there were many utopian schemes surfacing in Britain, with people wishing to buy properties and turn them into spiritual centres, influenced by the success of the Findhorn community in Scotland.

I was invited to join one such quest in 1974, proposed by New Age motivator Michael Riddell, who started a number of inspirational projects at that time. A group, mainly from Bath, began to look at properties that were for sale. These included a Victorian castle owned by the Wills (cigarette) family, St. Catherine's Court outside Bath, now owned by actress Jane Seymour and her husband, and several others. This questing would make a fine spiritual allegory and anecdote in itself, but we cannot explore it here!

As a result of my minor involvement in this project, I had some pivotal and powerful meetings with ARH at Castle House in Keinton Mandeville, near Glastonbury. My visits took place along with various friends and associates, including artist and musician Marko Galley, Rollo Maughling, and, of course, Michael Riddell. I later compared some of my experiences with others who had visited Heaver during the same period of the 1970's, including philosopher and author David Spangler, and Dorothy Maclean, one of the original founders of Findhorn, both being my friends and for a while, near neighbours.

The avowed intention of those visits to Keinton Mandeville was for the group to buy the Castle pub, a large property with gardens, that was conveniently close to Castle House, where Ronald Heaver had lived for some years. But for me, something entirely different happened.

Description of Ronald Heaver in the 1970's

ARH was an invalid, who had been stricken, as I was told, with paralysis many years before. Injuries to the spine and neck, by the way, form an important aspect of the inner teachings of the Grail Mystery, though most people shy away from this. His spinal injuries, as I was told, were first incurred as a pilot, defending Britain, then later re-occurred progressively in resonance with forces of change that brought Britain into the modern age. Like the Sacred Kings, he bore the burden for the people.

As a result he was a massive figure, who had been bed-ridden for some years when I met him. Prior to his becoming an invalid he had been a vigorous international traveler, an ace pilot, and had some remarkable spiritual experiences in several countries. He was on the fringe of the British "upper classes", though not extremely wealthy or privileged. ARH was of that generation of spiritual masters (now seemingly all departed from this world) who had a powerful sense of social grace and honourable class superiority, having been born in 1900 into a culture that we can barely imagine today.

In another historical world, of the past, he would have been a king or a high priest, and, indeed, he was both Priest and King, in the spiritual world of the present. He naturally commanded respect, and he expected his visitors to have both education and good manners. He was not patient with blunders or ignorance, though I must add that he was never short-tempered with me, despite his long years of severe physical disability and associated pain. Such vagaries of the emotions seemed unnecessary to him…"unnecessary" was a word that he used often. He once exorcised someone by simply saying "You can stop all that, now". And the possession stopped.

My First Visit and a Surprising Greeting!

On my first visit, in 1974, at age 25, I was nervous as I entered ARH's bedroom where he held audience, meeting from his bed with many people who visited, usually one at a time. I do not remember talking about the property scheme, which was the original intention. As I sat down, he looked at me, looked deep into me, looked right through me, for I was transparent to him, and suddenly starting talking about the Order of Melchizadek, as if it was a conversation that we had been sharing for years, old master to young neophyte. He had an uncanny ability to see into people and say something to awaken them. His first words to me were not "hello young man" or "pleased to meet you" but "Now, about this Order of Melchizadek, you cannot join unless you are already a member, for it exists out of time yet reaches into time into this world…and you must reach out in return…when you reach your hand upwards, another hand will grip yours and pull you up…"

In the 1980's I incorporated the spiritual process, the inner power, of this startling introductory statement from ARH, into my empowered visions of *The King in the Tree*, which are taught to all my Inner Temples Inner Convocation groups. When ARH said these words to me, he was not merely talking, but opening out the power itself, and sensing, probing, how I responded to it. Of course, I did not understand this so clearly at that time, but I could feel the spiritual resonance in the room as he spoke, and, being young and immature, I found such authority and focus somewhat disconcerting. It reminded me, amusingly now (but uncomfortably then!), of being in front of the headmaster at school, but in some higher spiritual octave.

So after a brief and baffling audience, in which ARH talked about the Order of Melchizadek as if I had always known about it, and simply needed to be reminded, pulled up straight, stood to attention, discouraged from shilly-shallying, and strictly focused on the job in hand, I was dismissed, politely but firmly. Nothing else was discussed at this time. I went home with my mind reeling, and my soul vibrant.

My Second Visit, and Reactions From W. G. Gray

On a later visit, ARH (we called him Mr. Heaver, of course, and never Ronald) candidly and quite casually revealed that his interest in the "spiritual centre" project was solely to provide ongoing support for his lady companion, Polly, as he knew that she would outlive him by some years. He regarded the project itself as unimportant, or at least, as something that we would have to do ourselves, with minimal involvement from him. At this time I was not aware of his early attempts to buy the Chalice Well property in Glastonbury, but in retrospect, I can see that he had let go of founding a spiritual center, and was focusing only on deep inner spiritual mediation. Please note, dear reader, this is spiritual Mediation, not meditation. At the time of my first meetings, he only had six years to live, and he knew this. By this phase of his life, he was mediating direct spiritual power, in a way that required few words and little outer form.

Several years after ARH's death, Gareth Knight and I met Polly Wood, ARH's companion, at a gathering in Glastonbury Town Hall. She talked to us briefly about her recent hip surgery, her continued life after ARH's death, and about a dispute over his writings and papers. I never saw her again after that day.

One of my other teachers in the early 1970's was William G. Gray, an eccentric and somewhat controversial figure, author, Qabalist, and ritual magician. His books were, and still are, influential in the development of new Hermetic Qabalah, ritual magic, and ancestral magic at ancient sites. One of Gray's books, *The Rollright Ritual*, published in the early 1970's, was far ahead of its time, and influenced many wiccans and pagans. But it was in another context altogether that I discovered that W. G. Gray had also met with Ronald Heaver. This context was, of course, the Order of Melchizadek.

W. G. Gray had received teachings and initiation into the inner Order in the 1920's from his own mentor, in a sacromagical lineage that traced back through France into Russia in the 18th and 19th century and earlier. In the early 1970's I, in turn, received this initiation from W. G. Gray.

ARH was the only person that I ever heard Bill Gray speak of with deep respect. Bill was known to be offensive and scathing about many people, often for the slightest of reasons, or for no reason at all other than sheer cussedness, but never toward ARH. Bill Gray was afraid of no one, and would not hesitate to be confrontational on matters that made me, a liberal 20-something-year-old, cringe with political correctness. It was, after all, the style of those older generation war-time occultists, who had all been military types. Today most people find this attitude offensive and questionable (just as I did, back then). But it did not detract from their spiritual power, insights, and commitment.

On several occasions Bill called ARH "one of the Old Ones" and referred to him as a "Senior Officer"…seemingly in the army sense, but really in terms of the Inner Order. Gray was surprised that I visited ARH; he saw it as a spiritual encounter that confirmed something…though he was often secretive when it came to such matters, like all the older generation occultists. Bill and his wife Roberta, (who was an astrologer in the days when all calculations were done by hand, not on computer), had visited the sanctuary at Castle House some years before. They said that, for them, "that tiny room felt like a vast Cathedral".

My Third Visit and an Initiatory Experience

On my third visit, I entered the audience room, and, without any social chit-chat, ARH immediately told me to go out of another door on the opposite side of the room, and on into the Sanctuary to meditate. This was a small building in the garden, very plain, with an eternal light burning over an otherwise empty altar . He gave me no clue what to do, or what to expect. I was told to stay for at least 15 minutes in complete silence, then report back to him. This was not an invitation, it was an order.

The method of teaching that ARH used was not verbal or textual training, such as we often expect today, but directly transmitted experience with no preliminaries that might get in the way. This is an ancient method of spiritual teaching. You are induced into the experience first, then you are tested on your experience by the master, and only then, if you are up to it, will you be "taught" anything in the way of details. The teaching is merely a verbal confirmation and expansion of your direct experience. Little or nothing is written down. As a result of ARH's powerful influence, I have tried to follow this method in my workshops, which contain material that is not found in my published work, and which cannot be communicated in print alone.

When I returned to the room, he questioned me about what I had sensed, felt, seen, and learned during my time alone in the Sanctuary. He was strict in this, and brooked no nonsense, fantasy, or uncertainty. I replied that I had a surprising vision of the Virgin holding a sheaf of wheat: he said, with little interest, as if I had stated something so obvious that it was hardly worth pursuing, "yes, yes, but what else?" I replied that next, after the vision of the Virgin, I had a feeling of radiant spiritual power of the Archangel Michael, but somehow attuned in a special way that I did not understand. Once again, this was taken for granted, as if it was widely known to all and rather obvious…he said, "Oh yes, yes, that is because we are on the Michael line that runs through the centre of the Earth and leads to Jerusalem…what else?" Unable to process this statement (though I understood it later) I said that towards the close of my meditation, I had found myself, for a brief moment, in a chamber or chapel of utter stillness and silence with many powerful, but dimly perceived presences watching me intently. This spirit chapel had become at one with the physical sanctuary in which I sat, and so I was in both places at once. "Aha!" he replied, for this was what ARH had been waiting for, and he proceeded to tell me more about the Order of Melchizadek and the spiritual Elders who keep Convocation in the chapel or inner sanctuary. This teaching has stayed with me through my life, and has been influential in my own work, writing, and public and private teaching.

This was the first time that I had been obliged to both reveal and assess some of my spiritual senses in the presence of a highly evolved master. With W. G. Gray, teaching was conducted through rambling, often evasive, conversations, and through bombardment with long intense rituals and ceremonies that were unquestionably powerful, but bordered on tedious. Heaver did none of this. As I mentioned above, I was in my mid-20s, and my debriefing, by ARH, of 15 minutes in the Sanctuary was an astonishing experience, which, in maybe no more than half an hour changed my life, and enabled me to trust and explore my spiritual senses further. I am still exploring them to this day.

The classic esoteric spiritual tradition that he described to me on after my visit to the Sanctuary at Castle House, has many variants worldwide, and became, in my own presentations of a perennial truth, the Chapel of the Elders, or the Sanctuary before the Void. I have taught this in many classes and experiential workshops, from 1988 to the present day. It forms an important part of my Inner Temple Traditions Inner Convocation series. You can find a guideline text for this Visionary Form in Appendix Four.

Having rather swiftly and surgically confirmed my spiritual sensitivities, ARH then suddenly jumped track (as it seemed, but maybe not) and told me the remarkable story about a talisman or thaumaturgal that he had buried in Jerusalem in the 1930s, and how many years later it had been found and returned to him in England. This is a famous story among British esotericists, and is part of the 20th century Glastonbury mythos. At that time I did not know what to make of it. Heaver seemed to be expecting some particular response or reaction from me, or perhaps he may have assumed that I would know the story already. In this I disappointed him, so he suddenly changed subject, talking next about duty and my allocated path in life. Certain duties were made very clear to me, at that time.

Nowadays I have better understanding of this true legend of the "traveling talisman", for it was a dramatic re-enactment, in real life, through the mysterious movement to and fro of both humans and talisman, of that same link between Jerusalem and England that was described in the 18th century by William Blake, in his poem Jerusalem. The verses were set to music by Parry, and are now famous, probably for the wrong reasons, as a "patriotic hymn" which is certainly very far from Blake's intention. If you practice Qabalah, as ARH certainly did, these verses are replete with multiple levels of meaning and spiritual inspiration.

And did those feet in ancient time
Walk upon England's mountains green?
And was the holy Lamb of God
On England's pleasant pastures seen?
And did the Countenance Divine
Shine forth upon our clouded hills?
And was Jerusalem builded here
Among these dark Satanic mills?
Bring me my bow of burning gold:
Bring me my arrows of desire:
Bring me my spear: O clouds unfold!
Bring me my chariot of fire.
I will not cease from mental fight,
Nor shall my sword sleep in my hand
Till we have built Jerusalem
In England's green and pleasant land.

This same mysterious theme was also described in a much earlier text, by the medieval poet Robert de Boron, in his story concerning Joseph of Arimathea and the two Vessels of Blood and Water (Seed) that were brought to Glastonbury. These Vessels were said to be the daughter and son of Jesus, by Mary Magdalene. I received the inner teaching, regarding the two Vessels, from W. G. Gray, and within his generation of British mystics and occultists it was regarded as one of the Sacred Mysteries that merged paganism and esoteric Christianity through the holy location of Glastonbury. Nowadays it is bandied about as some kind of idle sensationalist fiction. Of course there is much more to it than the obvious aspects, for it is not merely a legendary history, as it contains a practical method of spiritual transformation, that has be entered into, rather than merely read about. So while such modern popular fiction is somewhat offensive to members of the esoteric traditions, it is ultimately harmless and laughable.

ARH's remarkable and mysterious moving talisman was, in essence, this same story, this same power, at work in the 20th century, as it was all about the link between Britain and the Holy Land, the British soul and the Christ power. It took me many years to realize that the Heaver/Talisman story was part of an enduring spiritual continuum, and not merely an account of a one-off remarkable set of events.

Ronald Heaver, Dion Fortune, and Ritual Magic

At one point in our conversation, I asked ARH if he had known Dion Fortune, who had lived in Glastonbury and was buried in the town churchyard, and he laughed. "Oh yes, she was involved in ritual magic you know…totally unnecessary". I was pretty certain, at that time, that ritual magic was, indeed, necessary, but it was difficult to disagree with ARH, as he knew intuitively what was passing through your mind, was always several steps and jumps ahead of you, and every statement that he made was a spiritual teaching of some sort, that pulled you up, and made you think on a new level. Ten minutes with ARH was like ten hours of intense concentration or challenging physical exercise…except it was spiritual. Of course ritual magic is, indeed, no longer necessary once you have worked your way through its disciplines and arts, and emerged on the other side with a highly developed consciousness! That is what he was saying to me, back then in 1974, though I did not understand him at the time. It was certainly not necessary for ARH, who transformed all by being present, rather than by doing anything. This is the difference between direct spiritual mediation, and all the many techniques practiced today. ARH was a direct mediator, rather than a technician of spiritual methods.

A Theory of Telluric Energy Networks in the Earth

On my last visit of the mid-1970's, though not my ultimate meeting, as there was one more, he outlined in some detail a revolutionary esoteric theory of how ley lines (ever popular) were not straight lines along the surface of the land as is popularly taught, but that they pass down through the centre of the planet, then are deflected or reflected at various angles to link geomantic or telluric power sites that were thousands of miles apart on the surface. He likened this to the angular relationships in an astrological natal chart (the square, trine, sextile, and so forth). He told me that certain mountains in Tibet, in the Holy Land, and South America, had powerful angular relationships through the centre of the Earth, to one another, and of course, to Glastonbury Tor.

Looking back on this, I think that he sensed that I was soon to be working with UnderWorld spiritual forces that radiate from the planetary heart, and his remarkable intuition had led him to talk to me about this network of connections. In 2005 I took part in a private ritual with a Peruvian shaman, in which a traditional Peruvian teaching about linking mountains together, exactly mirrored what I had learned from ARH back in the 1970's, albeit with a different cultural ambience. This reminded me of the strong emphasis that ARH placed upon sacred mountains in South America, and their future role for the coming era of world transformation. In the past, he said, Tibet, but in the future, South America. This shift of power was clear, if you knew where the power-lines went as they passed through the center of the Earth.

Initiation and Transmission Handed on By Ronald Heaver

Not long before he died, ARH transferred the inner power of the priesthood to me, in a simple direct transmission, without ritual (of course!). This was, essentially, a Melchizadek initiation, similar to one I had received from W. G. Gray in a ritual lodge context, formally witnessed by Norman Gibbs a few years before, but with certain significant differences of inner contact and subtle power. It added something clear and catalyzing to the power that I had received from Gray, and this combined transmission is what I work with in the Consecration ceremonies, from time to time within my own groups.

I make no claim to having any special relationship with ARH. I am sure that I was just one (hopefully promising) young initiate that encountered him at this time. My sense, even now, is that he was a Priest of priests, more concerned with a vast overview of the spiritual evolutionary forces, than with training individuals. The training was through being in his presence, and you could take it or leave it.

Inner Temple Consecrations and Their Validity

It is most important to remember that this type of transmission, such as I received from both Gray and Heaver, is handed on by physical interaction and presence…it cannot be received or communicated unless you are in the presence of the master, as it is handed on while in the physical human world…it has long been known that the deep initiations are enabled by proximity, by touch, not by inner vision alone. There are also certain teachings and methods that are handed on, usually in a whisper. Without knowledge of these instructions, and without a special form of the sacred Touch not widely known, any claims to be able to initiate or consecrate are invalid. Of course, many groups and orders offer formal initiations into grades and membership, and that is an entirely different matter.

ARH died in 1980, so anyone claiming initiation from him must be able to confirm that they met him before that date. In the 1970's he held meetings with a number of people who are now known as spiritual teachers or innovators in various ways, and his influence was far reaching, despite his lack of public appearances. Any claims by people who did not meet him before his death must be highly questionable, and are likely to be false.

I attribute much of the inspiration for the deeper Inner Temple Traditions Inner Convocation material, not so much to W. G. Gray, but to the initiatory meetings and transmission that I received from Ronald Heaver back in the 1970's, at a time when my spiritual path was being revealed to me by some remarkable teachers.

Zadok, and the Death of Ronald Heaver

For some years ARH wrote letters, essays, and pamphlets under the pen-name Zadok, the priest. You can find insights into this theme in the Salomonic tradition of Qabalah. The Hebrew word also implies the term Justified, and it was ARH who first put me into contact with the inner spiritual order of Justified Men that I wrote about in my early book *The UnderWorld Initiation* (published 1985), and which I teach in the Inner Temple Traditions Inner Convocation work. The concept is an ancient one, found in many spiritual traditions in various forms, for it describes a collective of advanced spiritual awareness, to which we may attune in meditation

= TZZadik

and inner vision. This collective of consciousness is found both in the UnderWorld and in the OverWorld, where it is located, metaphysically, in the Chapel of the Elders or Sanctuary before the Void. I should add that the Order of Justified Men is not anything exclusively patriarchal: it is a collective term rather than a gender specific term. The old usage of "men" for a plural can mean "human", and comes from "manu" the hand, rather than from male gender. The Inner Temples, of course, include both priestesses and priests, as does the Sanctuary before the Void.

I was not present at ARH's death, but I was told by Rollo Maughling and several others that he died in full awareness at the local cottage hospital, having invited some friends and protegés to be present. His death was, I was told, peaceful and quiet, and he died on his 80th birthday.

So that is the story of my meetings with Ronald Heaver, meetings that exerted a powerful influence on me, and opened out certain specific inner teachings and contacts for me.

The spiritual centre? It never happened…but the idea and the resulting interactions seeded many other things into the minds and souls of those involved. That seeding is, of course, the true spiritual centre, the Temple built without hands.

Appendix 2
The Rising Light Below

This is a simple but major technique for arousing energy and passing it through your body: the power that rises from the UnderWorld, the Light within the Earth, will awaken and transform your own energies far more effectively than concentrating in isolation upon your power centers or chakras. If you do this exercise once every day and also work with visualization techniques on a regular basis, you will realign and activate your own energy centers rapidly.

This exercise is the mirror-working to those well-publicized techniques which call down light "from above". In both cases the energy seems to begin outside the individual (though this understanding changes as you develop your inner powers), but in this technique the light is inherent within the UnderWorld, often in a latent mode. Human awareness activates the power and draws it up through the body of the land into the human body. The Rising Light Below exercise is more effective while standing, though it may also be done sitting cross-legged, as squatting and cross-legged posture all enhance our Earth contact. Here are the stages, with some brief notes on their development and effect:

1. Begin with a period of silence and steady regular breathing. Your arms are lowered, with the fingertips stretched and pointing towards the ground. If you are sitting they may touch the ground lightly or rest upon your thighs. This initial arm position is important, as you will be raising your arms to different positions through the exercise.

2. Be aware of the point of contact between your body and the ground. If this is the floor of a room be aware that the building is in contact with the ground, with the land. For obvious reasons this type of exercise is enhanced by working directly upon the surface of the land, or in a cave, basement or underground chamber. By the holism, paradox, or "law" of reflections and octaves, it also works very well in high places, such as the tops of hills and in tall buildings. Many UnderWorld techniques are useful for those of us who live in a city environment, as they pass directly through the imbalanced enervating city energy field, which has little or no effect upon them. If you live in an unhealthy energy-isolated building, do this exercise on the roof or in the basement as well as in your own apartment.

3. Visualize a source of energy just below the ground or floor where your feet or body make contact. This is usually felt and seen as a flowing ball of light. The upper surface of this energy sphere touches the soles of your feet (or your legs, thigh and buttocks if you are sitting in a cross-legged position) and from it's lower surface a strand of light descends into the heart of the land, into the depths of the planet to an unknown source. This is your reflected energy field in the UnderWorld, normally latent. You are going to activate it, bring it alive through conscious work. Remember that it is part of you, reflected energy which you do not normally access or use, something of which millions of people are completely unaware, even those who practice meditation and energy techniques.

4. Increase your awareness of this energy sphere: feel it touching you, move your imagination into it. You may feel your personal energies descending into it, and a sensation of heat where your body touches the ground.

5. Gradually draw the energy source into yourself. This is done by breathing steadily and feeling the energy sphere rise through your feet into your body. You arm/hand position is slowly raised, drawing the energy with it. There are four zones of the body/energy field: **Feet/Genitals/Heart/Throat (Head)** (see Figure Four). These are our human reflection of the holism of the Elements and Worlds.

6. **Feet**: be aware of the Element of Earth, and the matter or substance of your entire body. The energy sphere rises up through your feet, legs and thighs. This is the first awakening of energy within

your physical substance. Your arms are still directed downwards, but slowly raised, drawing the energy as they move.

7. **Genitals**: be aware of the Element of Water, and the twofold nature of water in your body. Firstly it is the fundamental element of your cells; on a non-physical level Water is the element of creation, birth, sexual union, love, and represents the second awakening of energy within your physical substance. Your arms are raised gradually to waist height.

8. **Heart**: be aware of the Element of Fire. As the energy sphere rises, it gradually becomes more incandescent. The Four Elements

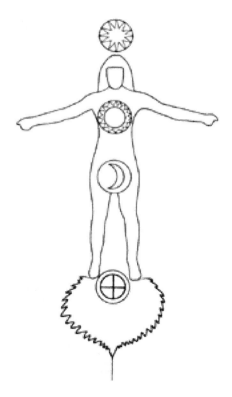

Figure 4: The Rising Light

are simultaneously literal and metaphysical. At this heart level the increasing rate of your energy becomes fire. In your body this is bio-electrical energy, the flow of blood and the subtle forces that radiate from your life core. As these subtle forces manifest they appear in an increasingly watery and earthy form. The incandescence of the energy sphere rising from the UnderWorld through your body is the third awakening of energy within your physical substance. Your arms are raised, palms upward, to shoulder height.

9. **Throat**: be aware of the Element of Air. The energy has now risen to surround your head and shoulders, and has reached its most rapid and mobile rate. All four zones are now alive, each rising level through the body being holistically within one another. Yet the elevation of energy towards the head causes an increase in rate, and changes of your consciousness. Your arms are raised above the head, palms upwards.

10. Returning the power. Simply reverse the sequence by steadily lowering your arms and feeling the power pass down through your body. It returns steadily to your energy sphere within the land, below your feet. As it descends, you lower your arms, and each of the four zones gently reduces in activity.

Appendix 3
The Stillness Form
(from The Inner Temple Traditions)

Form1: The Stillness Form

The Stillness Form is Form (1) of a series of visionary forms that comprises the basic Inner Temple Inner Convocation foundation training. The other four Forms are included in Appendix Four. For work with the Sphere of Art, this Stillness Form, and the act of Becoming Void, are essential training. Therefore this Form has been included as a separate appendix.

This Form has been published in several versions in many of my books between 1987 and the present year, as it is an essential prerequisite to any meditation, visualization, or magical work, be it solo or in a group context. (Versions of this Form can be found in *Living Magical Arts* (1987/2007), *Advanced Magical Arts* (1988/2007), *Music and the Elemental Psyche* (1987), *Music Power Harmony* (1988), *Dreampower Tarot* (1990), *The Miracle Tree* (2003), and other books in various editions and translations worldwide). This basic Form has been taught at my workshops and classes from 1989 to the present day, and all students and group members use it to begin their meditations and inner work.

There are "hidden" aspects to this Form which are taught to our advanced students, and to those teachers that I have trained. These will not be published, but can be learned and experienced in the advanced workshops and classes.

Recommendation: You can practice this Form in its own right without other stages, and this is the best way to develop your skill at

Entering Stillness. You should also use this before and after each and any type of spiritual/magical work that you undertake.

1. Breathing steadily align yourself to the Directions: Above, Below, Within. Then: East, South, West, North. Then: Before you, Behind you, to your Right, to your Left…and the centre within.

2. Still your sense of Time, of Space, and of Movement. Breath steadily, letting go of Time, Space, and Movement.

3. Reach into the Stillness Within, beyond all time, space, and movement.

4. Chant the vowel sound OAI three times, elongating the vowels on one steady tone. The "O" stills Time. The "A" draws in Space to the centre. The "I" stills all movement.

5. Be Still. Reach into the Void of Un-being, out of which all Being comes.

6. Affirm again the Directions.

7. Close your meditation and return to the outer world. *Or* proceed with your intended spiritual/magical/meditational working, bringing it to life out of the Stillness.

Appendix 4
Four Further Forms
(from The Inner Temple Traditions)

Form 2: The Timeless Inner Convocation

This Form 2 is a refinement and update of the basic method of moving into the Timeless Convocation and Inner Temples.[23] I have been teaching this Form, and the related Inner Temple Traditions Inner Convocation series, since 1989 in both Britain and the USA. Many groups use an earlier version of these visionary meditations or Forms. The technique is ancient, as it describes a real place and condition of consciousness, and has parallels in many traditions worldwide. In keeping with the aim of my *Magical Arts* series books, this is a modern version, developed from experience and from inner contacts to be rapidly effective. Five to ten minutes of this Form each day will make profound changes to your awareness.

1. Be still, stilling your sense of time, space, and movement. (light a candle)

2. Let your awareness rest upon the candle flame, and know that this terrestrial fire of earth and moon is at one with the celestial fire of sun and stars. Feel your own flame of being within, resonate with the candle flame. The flame expands and grows and becomes a pillar of light, extending to the heights above and to the depths below.

3. With this awareness, pass through into the Timeless Convocation, a perpetual communion of many beings at the threshold of the void, where the flame of being becomes a pillar of light extending through the universe. Be still here, and rest in communion with the

spiritual presence of this timeless place, known through the ages to all that seek spiritual communion and enlightenment.

4. Now be aware again of the room or place around you, above, below, and within. Know that this too, is the Pillar of Light and the Timeless Convocation. Let your sense of the regenerative power of the convocation flow out to the outer world.

5. Now return to your outer awareness, and go in peace. (gently put the candle out, or leave it to burn safely on your altar)

Form 3: Working With The Four Temples

You can use this Form 3 in five separate parts for short meditations/visions (East one, South two, West three, North four, Center five) or use the entire form from beginning to end, which is the recommended method. Before working with this spiritual Form 3, either in parts or entire, always use Form 1 for entering Silence.

In the East, the Temple of Instruction and Inspiration

In the South, the Temple of Initiation and Illumination

In the West, the Temple of the Ebbing and Flowing Tides

In the North, the Temple of Destruction and Regeneration

From the East, the Temple of Instruction and Inspiration mediates the spiritual powers of Life and the elemental energy of Air

From the South, the Temple of Initiation and Illumination mediates the spiritual powers of Light and the elemental energy of Fire

From the West, the Temple of the Ebbing and Flowing Tides mediates the spiritual powers of Love, and the elemental energy of Water

From the North, the Temple of Destruction and Regeneration mediates the spiritual powers of Law, and the elemental energy of Earth.

Each Temple has three zones, three courts, three deepening states of Being.

East

The outer court of the East offers Instruction in skills, arts, sciences of magic, of invention, of healing techniques, of music, of words, of mathematics and sacred geometry. All the skills that make civilization are mediated in this outer court of the East, and all the methods of sacro-magical arts are taught here. Its mysterious life power streams through the air that flows in and out of our lungs, and can be expressed through honorable speech and inspiring words. Many temples and religions of the outer world have been seeded from this Inner Temple through the ages. (pause here for silent meditation)

The middle court of the East contains the deities of human culture: those gods and goddesses of the ancestral traditions that teach and mentor humanity, that bring honor, discipline, clarity of awareness, and foster communication. All messenger deities are here, all gods and goddesses of Honour and the spiritual martial arts, powers of justice, powers of healing. They take many forms and have many names, but they all embody the powers of Instruction and Inspiration that move out into manifestation. Here in this middle court, work with them in your chosen form. (pause here for silent communion or ritual pattern)

The inner court of the East is the place of Living Spirit. Where the First Breath of Being whispers out of the Void, and utters the First Word of Cosmos. Be still, and feel that Breath of Being within you, merge with the Living Spirit in the sanctuary of the Temple of Life. (pause here for contemplation and communion)

South

The outer court of the South offers Initiation into energetic and spiritual growth, transformation, and subtle forces of the Inner Fire. It creates the energy that flows through the skills, arts, and disciplines formed by the Temple of the East, and its subtle fire radiates through our blood. Its mysterious initiatory power brings changes in our lives, and in the life of humanity, and in the life of our planet Earth. Its current of energy radiates through all forms, galvanizing them into movement. In ancient times this was our ancestral Fire Temple, source of the priest and priesteshood of Light and Fire in the human world. Today there are few temples and religions in the outer world that manifest this power. (pause here for silent meditation)

The middle court of the South contains the deities of fire and light, which take many forms and have many names through the ages. All solar and light bearing gods and goddesses are here, all deities of balance and harmony, embodying the energies of Initiation and Illumination that radiate to the outer world. Here in this middle court, work with them in your chosen form. (pause here for silent communion or ritual pattern.)

The inner court of the South is the place of Limitless Light. Where the Light of Being flows out of the primal Darkness of the Void, and Illuminates Creation. Be still, and feel the Light within you merge with the Light of the sanctuary of the Inner Temple of Light. (pause here for contemplation and communion)

West

The outer court of the West offers the flowing tides of Giving and Receiving. It provides the ebb and flow of compassionate communion through all living beings. Its tides wash us clean, and nourish us anew. All life on Earth begins in the ocean and the Sea Temple communes its power to us through the water in our bodies and the purified emotions of our souls. (pause here for silent meditation)

The middle court of the West contains the gods and goddesses of love compassion and empathy that have taken many forms in our world through the ages. They embody and mediate the forces of ocean: ocean of water, ocean of stars, and they Give and Receive our most pure love flowing in and out of all that lives. Here in this middle court, work with them in your chosen form. (pause here for silent communion or ritual pattern)

The inner court of the West is the place of Perfect Love, where the sacred vessel pours forth the limitless Love of Being that flows out of, and into, the Void. Here is where vast waters of Cosmos pour forth into infinite worlds, and here is the place to which they return. Perfect Love at Peace is the power of this sanctuary, which is found in the place where all tides become Still. Feel your innermost love of all being, merge with the Perfect Being of Love in the sanctuary of this Inner Temple of Love. (pause here for contemplation and communion)

North

The outer court of the North offers the mysteries of coming into Form and of going into Formlessness. This is the place of destruction and regeneration, where old patterns are broken down, that they may make the ground for new seeds to grow within us. It provides the subtle forces that reduce and liberate, for the laws of life are also laws of liberation. Here are the mysteries of deepest night and death discovered, through understanding manifestation and return to spirit. Here the sacred mysteries of Earth are revealed. (pause here for silent meditation)

The middle court of the North contains the deities that destroy and purify, the dark powers that draw all unto themselves, in order that all may be reborn. They embody the ultimate transformations that are available to all forms, all life, and all entities. Here are all gods and goddesses of night, of the UnderWorld, of death, of the hidden Crossroads between the worlds. They bring you strength through your bones, through the bones of planet Earth. Here in this middle court, work with them in your chosen form. (pause here for silent communion or ritual pattern)

The inner court of the North holds the mystery of Grace, and the wisdom of Spirit utterly present in Substance. Here is where the sacred Stone is buried deep in the UnderWorld, at the very threshold of the Void. Commune now with this power in your bones, in the sanctuary of this Inner Temple of cosmic Law. (pause here for contemplation and communion)

Center

In the Centre is the Flame of Being, appearing as a Pillar of Light that extends to the height above and descends to the depth below. And at its Centre is that beautifying redeeming transformation power that is at the heart of all things yet is bound by none.

Life Light Love and Law come together in the Pillar of Light, merging and emerging out of the Truth of Being, the Centre of Cosmos.

Be Still, and be At One with the central Flame of Being, the Pillar of Light. (pause here for contemplation and communion)

Returning to the Outer World

Be aware that you are in the Inner Convocation. Know that you may return here in your dreams visions and meditations. Now be aware of the outer temple, of the sky above and the land below. And be aware of the directions before you, behind you, to your right, to your left, above, below, and within. Know that the Inner Temples and the outer world come together as One, through your body.

Now depart in Peace.

Form 4: The Library of the Inner Convocation (part 1)

Background and History of "The Library"

This visionary form is, in essence, a unique version of one of the best known visualizations of the Western esoteric tradition. I have taught this method in the UK and the USA from 1987 to the present day. Early workings with the Inner Convocation and the Library in the UK were included at private meetings at my house in Bath, in the 1980's, with various members including Gareth Knight, John and Caitlin Matthews, Marion Green and Richard Swettenham. From the late 1980's the Inner Library formed part of the basic Inner Temple Traditions Inner Convocation material that I have taught publicly to may students in the USA, Canada, and Britain

The concept of a spiritual "Library" was widely taught and practiced in all the older magical lodges, and has significant parallels in Qabalistic and Sufi mysticism. There are many variants of this form, in private circulation and in publication. Dion Fortune describes the Library in her books and in more detail in her papers from the 1930's, (now edited and published by Gareth Knight) and it is found (of course) in the 19th century writings of Madam Blavatsky, such as *Isis Unveiled* and *The Secret Doctrine*. It is Blavatsky to whom we should credit the origins of the popular idea of the "akashic records", borrowed and adapted creatively from Buddhist tradition. The Library and the Records are virtually synonymous in modern popular practice, though a detailed analysis, and deeper exploration, soon reveal that the Library is a spiritual location or place, while the Records may be found in that place, but are not the Library itself. We will return to this idea shortly, when we explore the nature and reality of the Library.

I first experienced the Library in 1971 while working with W. G. and Roberta Gray (Bill and Bobby), at their home in Cheltenham. Bill introduced me to the Library in a guided vision, a standard version used by many teachers and occultists of the older generation. This widely taught vision of The Library is the foundation for my own work, though I have made many changes according to my own insights and experience, and created a new text integrated with my overall Inner Temple Traditions Inner Convocation work. As a result of my first encounter with the Library, back in 1971, I discovered that, among other things, it can contain and reveal accurate details of the future. Here is what happened:

Bobby, who was a science-fiction writer in addition to being an astrologer and Celtic scholar, told me this (in 1971): "What I look for in the Library are the little silver discs, like circular mirrors, that you post into a slot, like a letter box, and anything you want to study comes up on a TV screen. Don't think that the Library is limited to antique scrolls, the ways of the future are there too!" At this time, personal computers were unknown in general use, and the CD ROM had not yet appeared. When I was shown an audio CD a few years later, while recording film music for the BBC, I was astounded to realize that this was the technology of communication that Bobby Gray had seen in the Inner Library. Shortly after audio CDs, I saw such "little silver discs" linked to information displayed on a visual screen, on a home computer, the familiar data and program CDs which we all use now. Yet Roberta Gray had seen this technology, and used it, in the Inner Library in the 1960's and earlier, years before it manifested in outer form.

Such future-vision is not, of course, the main purpose of entering the Library, but Bobby's story serves as a historical moment, of my own introduction to the Library, and beginning to work with it in the early 1970's. When teaching this visionary Form to students, from 1987 onwards, I have often recounted this story as a way of introducing the idea, and demonstrating its potential.

What is the Library?

The Library is a presentation, a visionary model or interface, of the Universal Mind, associated with the 6th Sphere of the Tree of Life, a spiritual consciousness of knowledge centrality, relationship, and harmony. It is the place in which past and future merge together in the time-free present, and thus it is a storehouse of transcendent and trans-temporal Knowledge.

In association with the Inner Temple Traditions Inner Convocation, the Library becomes a focused inner-world place. Priests and Priestesses have been using the Library, in various forms, for thousands of years. Before we progress to our visionary Form for entering the Library, some basic concepts will be helpful to the reader, student, and practitioner, intending to work seriously with this Form.

The Structure of the Library

The Library is a spiritual location, a place and state of consciousness and energy. In the esoteric traditions the body, vessel, or "building" of the library is an ark formed of angelic beings. They constitute the collective form, the energetic field or shell that holds the content. These angels are, specifically, those that record, observe, know, communicate, and hold in balanced motion. (If you know Hebrew, each of these angelic functions is also the name of an order of angels on the Tree of Life, which you will recognize).

The Content of the Library

Within the angelic structure of Recording, Observation, Knowledge, Communication, and Holding in Balance, that comprises the vessel or ark of the Library, is the originally empty space of the interior. This is imminent knowledge, which gradually becomes manifest. It becomes manifest partly through interaction with time, and partly through interaction with consciousness. We interpret that manifestation historically, as books, scrolls, engravings, communications technology, and so forth. For us knowledge manifests as information in the outer world, but the Library holds deeper modes of knowledge that we can also access with practice, knowledge before information, and knowledge beyond information.

Over millenniums, the empty vault of the Library, the vessel of imminent knowledge, becomes shaped and defined through interaction. In other words, the Library fills up. The most significant interaction for us, as humans, is that which arises when individuated consciousness enters the Library. In our general experience, the consciousness that enters the library is often human or transhuman, but many other beings also use the Library. The long practice of going there in meditation, especially among priests priestesses and initiates, has built a reservoir of energy and consciousness in the vessel, in the Library. Thus, when we use a traditionally based vision, that of a grand building with many books, scrolls, and other forms of recording and communication, we are using such historical stereotypes as an interface for relationship with Knowledge. When we enter the Library at a deeper level of awareness, we also find other forms therein...sometimes those of the technological future, and often those of the organic libraries of life-forms in nature. Occasionally we may encounter beings that are completely "other" in their nature, though this is relatively unusual.

In the Library we do not merely study books: the popular, and highly reduced and simplistic idea of the "akashic records" is often modeled as reading a book...every spiritualist medium and channeller knows how to present or to pretend a version of this "reading the records", though usually without the context or deeper contact of the Library. There is much more to the Library than is known in the popular themes of the Records.

In the Library, we may meet inner plane beings, just as we do in the Temples and the Inner Convocation. With practice, the Library becomes a meeting place for sharing, giving and receiving, knowledge. It is, in fact, a higher octave of the Crossroads that is used in folkloric faery and UnderWorld magic, whereby humans meet spirit beings and exchange with them.

Being a Crossroads, the Library also acts as an interim place, a consubstantial locus in which the edges or thresholds of many other loci (spiritual places) merge together. Traditionally these are envisioned as halls, chamber, chapels, shrines, rooms, corridors leading in and out, and so forth.

Students of classical history and culture will recognize connections to the Theatre of Memory that was used by the orators of the Roman and Greek world... a mnemonic system that built an amphitheatre and temples in the mind, to store and rearrange information. This method derives directly from the older temple arts of memory which were practiced in the Library for sacromagical purposes.

Why Do We Go to the Library?

In the basic training known to every lodge member or Western tradition student, the Library is taught early on. It is still one of the basic introductory forms that I teach to all Inner Temple students or new group members, and have done so since 1987. This is because its outer levels, the most accessible, can provide the student with a resource for learning. You can learn anything you want in the Library, plus many things that you had no idea might be relevant to you. Often the practice of using the Library stops at this level, and goes no further. As mentioned above, the popular notion of the "akashic records" is the most superficial level of accessing the Library…usually attempted without any knowledge of the real nature of the Library itself.

Repeated use of the Library, in an informed and dedicated manner, coming and going, studying and learning, gradually opens out certain innate inner abilities, potentials of consciousness, perception, reception, that we all have within us. Such abilities are enhanced and amplified by the Inner Temple techniques acquired through our other Forms, such as Entering Stillness, the Pillar of Light, and Experience of the Four Temples.

The Library also provides an interface, within its visionary scenario, for communication between the outer world and the occupants of the Inner Temples. They will teach us things in the Library, and find appropriate ways of communicating with us, through the long standing patterns of consciousness-exchange stored in the Library.

Finally, the Library leads to some deeper spiritual realms of awareness, due to its Crossroads function. We will explore these deeper realms elsewhere, in our other Inner Temple Inner Convocation Forms.

Form 4: The Library of the Inner Convocation (part 2)
Experiencing the Library

Begin with Silence (See Form 1)

Light a candle flame, or alternatively, use a bowl of spring water or a stone as your focus point. Make your vow and state clearly your reason for seeking to enter the Library.

Be aware of a door of flame, appearing before you, guarded by fiery serpents with many eyes and many wings.

There are three steps up to the door, and as you approach the door, the guardians see deep into your heart and mind. If you have anything to hide, any ulterior motive for seeking this place of power, turn back now, for a deceitful heart and dishonest mind will draw the guardian powers against you. If your heart is pure, and your intentions selfless, pass through in peace, and be welcome.

Pass through into a long corridor with soaring arches. It leads to a central hall, where you sense see and feel many other corridors converging from all directions.

At the centre of the hall, under a high dome engraved with a pattern of stars, is an altar in the shape of an eagle with wide out-stretched wings, supported by two mighty bulls, one under each foot. See, sense, and feel the altar and the dome of stars. The stars move slowly in a sweeping curve around the dome.

Be aware that you are in the Inner Library, where all thought and knowledge come together beyond time. The Library is the Crossroads of time, space, and interaction. Priests and Priestesses of the Inner Temples come to this sacred location both to teach and to learn. You may discover much in this Library, about the cosmos, and about your true self. Know that you may return here in your dreams visions and meditations, and that the Library is always open to you. Know yourself, and you shall know the cosmos.

Look around you: you see many high galleries with books, scrolls, carved stones, inscribed metal plates, woven patterns, sculptures, pictures. You also see the technology of the remote past and of the future, all media of communication and learning are found here. Down certain long corridors you see living beings, some are the plants and organisms of your own world, and others are strange and utterly unknown to you. Each of these is a library in itself, if you learn how to merge with them and share their innate knowledge.

At this most ancient altar, brought here in spirit from our original temples on Earth that are long since lost, you reaffirm the vow that you made before the guardians of the doorway.

Be Still, and commune in silence, here at the very centre of the Library of the Inner Convocation.

(1st Silent Communion here)

Gradually you become aware of the structure and form of the library: at first it seems like a vast gothic building, but now it seems like a crystalline forest. Again it changes, and you discover that the pillars, curves, and dome, are made of many angelic beings, shaped and merged together in a huge network of connections. The vessel of the Library, its vast soaring structure that intersects many worlds, is a composite of those angels who watch, record, understand, and balance, the knowledge and wisdom of the cosmos.

Be Still, and come into their presence. By doing so, you become the Inner Library, through your body.

(2nd Silent Communion here)

Now you become aware of the Inner Light. It begins as a radiant flame upon the altar of the Eagle and Bulls. Within you, the inner fire rises in harmony with the altar flame. Your Inner Light increases and permeates your entire being. Be still, and be at one with the Inner Light.

(3rd Silent Communion here)

Be aware that you are in the central hall of the Inner Library, beneath the dome of living stars, at the foot of the altar of the Eagle and Bulls. Sense how the inner flame within you resonates with the altar flame, and know that you have been in this sacred place many times in many lives.

Now it is time to return to the outer world. Set in the far wall, see a small plain door, one of many. This is your way back to the human world, and it resonates with your birth, and your natal solar chart. When it opens you see yourself, in a pale shadowy place that seems momentarily unreal. Now you discover that this pale place is the outer world, the place where you began your vision of the Library. Pass through, and return to your outer self. Now the outer world solidifies, and you remember it once more.

Acknowledge the Directions of East South West and North, Above Below and Within, and sense that the hidden door closes behind you. Be at Peace, and carry your new knowledge within you as you live and work in the outer world of time, space, and movement.

(extinguish the candle flame gently, or pour away the water, or cover the stone with a cloth)

Form 5: The Chapel of the Elders.
(Also known as The Sanctuary Before the Void)

Introduction

I have worked with this material in my published writing from the 1980's to the present day, and have taught it in my Inner Temple

Traditions Inner Convocation classes to many students. My introduction to it was in the 1970's, as I describe shortly.

As with much of the Inner Temple Traditions Inner Convocation material, this visionary form has many historical and esoteric
precedents. It has been taught in the older magical lodges for generations, and is found in various presentations in many mystical
and magical traditions. There are parallels in Christian and Islamic
mystical practices, and in Jewish and Sufi Qabalah. There are also
significant parallels in Buddhist tradition, which are described later
in this Introduction.

Some of my older generation mentors were especially involved in
this method of spiritual communion, which they invariably linked
to the inner Order of Melchizadek. Sadly this noble and ancient
concept has been ruthlessly trivialized during the last 20 years or so,
especially in the New Age movements, but its spiritual origins are
still valid, no matter what has been done with it in public.

My introduction to this theme and to the power of the Sanctuary before the Void was in 1974, when instructed to go into a physical temple/sanctuary and meditate, under the guidance of the late
Ronald Heaver, while visiting him in his home. In Ronald Heaver's
sanctuary, a small very plain building with an eternal flame burning,
I came into the Sanctuary before the Void. Heaver later questioned
me very strictly on what I had experienced, and gave me a number
of teachings regarding the Order of Melchizadek. A few years before, I had received similar insights and material from W G Gray,
but Heaver brought an especial authority and inner contact from
the Order of Melchizadek. W G Gray regarded Ronald Heaver as a
"senior officer", using both British military terms, and those of the
formal Lodge. He accorded Heaver great respect.

The Sanctuary in Esoteric Tradition

While I often use the phrase "Sanctuary before the Void" another term for this collective of advanced spiritual consciousness
that is found in many sources is the Chapel of the Elders. Unfortunately for us today, this term may have some religious connotations
that people are uncomfortable with, especially as the same theme
can arise in various types of fundamentalism. However, what we are

concerned with here is spiritual reality, not political religion. The "elders" are not ancient bearded males, but a focused convocation of highly advanced consciousness, often appearing to the inner senses as priests and priestesses, from many sources and traditions, but beyond all cultural religion. They are transhuman beings, a subject that I have discussed in several of my books (including *Living Magical Arts* and *Advanced Magical Arts* published in 1987 and 1988, and *The Miracle Tree* published in 2003).

In a very broad sense, the spiritual power here is similar to that of the Bodhisattvas in Buddhist tradition. These are beings of intense spiritual awareness that remain in conclave at the very threshold of the Void, and are especially involved in mediating Compassion and Transformation. The purpose of such mediation, such dedication, is to consciously radiate spiritual powers out towards the many manifest worlds…including our own planet Earth.

We can detect and attune another parallel presentation in the Rosicrucian Vault, in which the elders are described as "sleeping" under an eternal light, guarding certain texts and sacred truths, which will be disseminated to the outer world. The Rosicrucian tradition is founded on Germanic/Teutonic faery tradition, with many Faery, UnderWorld, and Sacred Sleeper motifs, but fused creatively with a powerful protestant Christian initiatory impulse, plus images and practices from the ancient Mysteries of the classical world. Thus it is not surprising that a fusion of three powerful spiritual impulses should constellate around the Vault or Chapel of the Elders.

In our Inner Temples work, we are primarily concerned, as is right and proper for us, with planet Earth, and with concepts of service, compassion, and spiritual regeneration. The Sanctuary before the Void, also called the Chapel of the Elders, is a means whereby we can work towards such service.

Origins of This Text and Spiritual Practice

This spiritual "place" is sought by many mystical and ritual traditions, so my claim is to my own teachings and texts over the last 20 years or so, from 1987 to the present year, and not to the overview or concept, as this is a universal spiritual source. I have had the honor of communicating this spiritual presence, of the Sanctuary and the Elders, to hundreds of people over the years, and the deep privilege of sharing this with, and originally learning it directly from, a lineage of Western Tradition masters in the outer world during the 1970's. My mediation of this aspect of the Inner Order was received direct from my teachers, through the initiatory transmissions that are handed on only by specific Touch, and supported by "whispered wisdom", the line of teachings that are given by the master when the initiate has proven that he or she has truly entered the Sanctuary. This lineage is said to extend for thousands of years in historical time, and there are many recondite traditions and teachings associated with it.

My intention has been to make this, along with my other Inner Temple Traditions Inner Convocation workings, simple and accessible, and to offer ways of coming into the presence of the "Elders" that assist in our spiritual growth and transformation. At a later stage, after coming into their presence, we can discover the tasks and spiritual work that are allocated to us in the Sanctuary before the Void. This advanced level cannot be communicated by a written text, but is transmitted direct.

The Chapel Of The Elders
The Sanctuary Before The Void

Be Still, stilling Time Space and Movement. Chant OAI, if you are familiar with this method of stilling awareness.

Affirm the sacred directions: Above, Below, East South West and North, and Within.

Light a candle flame on your altar to embody the celestial fire manifest here on Earth.

Here you may use the Library empowered vision, which is our Form 4, as a means of accessing the chapel, or you may proceed as follows:

Sense see and feel that you pass through a door of flame that opens from the candle flame, and down a long corridor. (You may do this from within the Library if you wish, as in (4) above). Your sense of this corridor is of soaring arches with glimpses of stars beyond. Let your sight rest upon the sacred candle flame as you do this.

Build strongly before you the image of an ornately carved low door. Sense see and feel that you knock three times upon it. (At this point you may physically knock or gently stamp your foot here, which is a traditional practice at spiritual thresholds). The door opens, and you pass within.

First you perceive the altar at the far end of the Sanctuary: there is a simple flame burning upon a large altar. Beyond the altar is the Void, out of which all Being comes.

Next you sense, see, and feel, that there are many others in this chapel or sanctuary. Their presence may be felt more than seen. These are the elders or highly advanced priestesses and priests of many spiritual traditions that work here ceaselessly before the Void. Come into a silent communion with them. (Pause and be still here)

Now you are invited to pass to the altar, and stand with the Void behind you, and the altar before you. (If you have set up a simple altar in the outer world, take this position behind your candle flame, if possible. If necessary, rehearse this movement before you do the inner form, so that you are familiar with it).

Be Still, stilling Time, Space, and Movement. Sense how your inner Stillness allows the Infinite Potential behind you to flow through you. In your inner vision place your hands palm downwards upon the altar. (If possible do this in the outer world also).

To you now comes a Priest or Priestess from the assembled Elders, and he or she places their hands over yours. Be still, and commune in Silence now.

(after the Silence) be aware that you are in the Sanctuary before the Void, and that you may return here in your dreams, visions, and meditations. Form a clear intention in your mind that you are here in service to spiritual awareness, to the evolutionary forces of the Inner Temples, and that you ask nothing for yourself alone.

Sense see and feel now that the elder removes his or her hands from yours, and you pass around the altar to stand before it, facing into the chapel (do this physically if you can, with your altar and candle flame behind you). Sense see and feel the many beings that gather here.

Pass out of the Sanctuary before the Void, between two lines of priests and priestesses to your right and to your left, and then through the door. Be aware that you carry the spiritual power out into the outer world. (You may return to the Library, Form 4, at this stage if you wish, before returning to outer awareness)

Return to your outer awareness, sensing the Sky above, the Land below, and the Directions Before, Behind, Right and Left. Gently put out the candle, and close your working with the Sanctuary before the Void, the Chapel of the Elders.

(Write any notes or sensations or experiences if you wish, before doing anything else)

Note: This basic method has been taught to many people in my Inner Temple groups, and has been practiced in various forms, for many centuries. Therefore it has considerable psychic impetus and a deep imprint in the collective consciousness and the etheric (sublunar) mantle of our planet. It leads us to a real state of shared consciousness, which in turn will mediate, through us, transformative and regenerative spiritual power from the inner dimensions to the outer. Use it sparingly, and after each communion, allow time for the inner powers to manifest in your dreams, visions, and meditations.

Appendix 5
The Cover Illustration

Our cover illustration is taken from the *Musaeum Hermeticum*, a compendium of alchemical texts and images first published in 1652, with subsequent editions. Such emblems were widespread in alchemical literature, and were intended as "master keys" not merely to support text (which is typically the purpose of contemporary illustrations) but to transcend the text, acting as sources of direct insight during contemplation. When accessed in this manner, the alchemical emblems awaken as living visions, and hold many potential insights and realizations.

There are two standard contemporary ways of interpreting an alchemical emblem…one is a materialistic approach that describes alchemy as pseudo-scientific or kind of proto-chemistry or neo-physics, while the other is a psychological interpretation, also essentially materialistic, assuming that the alchemical transformations described are crude descriptions of psychic or mental/emotional processes within the individual. Neither of these interpretations are offered here, as they are both inadequate. In our context, the cover illustration is interpreted as a demonstration of the esoteric structure and operation of the Sphere of Art: it shows a pattern of subtle forces of energy and consciousness, and, reaching further, provides clues to a practical method of transformation. Such transformation is more than a merely psychological process or an alternative approach to chemistry.

Within and Without the Sphere

The emblematic picture shows the Sphere of Art extending above into the starry OverWorld and below into starry UnderWorld. Beyond the circumference of the Sphere the influence of the all-pervading Four Elements - Air/Fire/Water/Earth, is shown. The Elements are represented by traditional emblems: the winds for air, the salamander for fire, ships at sea for water, and a landscape for earth. The Sphere itself is defined by two hemispheres: the upper is a light hemisphere, the lower is a dark hemisphere, for the over and under worlds respectively. In each are shown the traditional images of the Seven Luminaries : Sun and Moon, with five stars/planets, representing Mercury, Venus, Mars, Jupiter, and Saturn. We will find this sequence mirrored inside the earth, beneath the hill.

The Sphere of Art is a reflection or miniature of the greater cosmos. The Four Elements are the active expressions, in the world of nature, of Four Primal Powers of Life/Light/Love/Law that emerge from the Void, as both the source and the ground of all manifestation.

On the Hill Top

Seated on the hill are three figures, traditionally representing initiates or adepts of alchemical and magical art that consciously unite the powers of above and below: these figures may be understood, however, at a deeper level as Male, Female, and Androgyne. The figure on the left is male, holding an upward pointing triangle that represents the Rising Light from the center of the Earth, or telluric and ascending consciousness/energy. This figure mediates the Evolutionary stream. That on the right is female, holding a downward pointing triangle that represents the Descending Light from the Stars, or stellar and planetary descending consciousness/energy. This figure mediates the Involutionary Stream. The central figure, which is androgyne, combines the Evolutionary and Involutionary, the telluric and the stellar, through the Hexagram.

It is through the union or sacred marriage of those ascending and descending powers that a New Sun is created in the center – as shown by the Hexagram. From within this New Sun the power of the Aesch Mezareph or Purifying Fire emerges. Through our Sphere of Art practices we discover that this New Sun is a power of fusion rather than of fission.

Beneath the Hill

Beneath the hill are the Elders seated in silent communion within the Underworld, a motif found in both faery tradition and Rosicrucian mysticism. Before them is a well that leads deeper into the Mystery of the UnderWorld. This is the Well of Light found in UnderWorld and faery traditions worldwide, which can be opened through a specific practice to admit the Rising Light Below. At a deeper level of interpretation, the figures beneath the hill are the seven luminaries, the Sun, Moon, Mercury, Venus, Mars, Jupiter and Saturn, embodied within the elements and metals, Gold, Silver, Quicksilver, Copper, Iron, Tin, and Lead. The figure holding a lyre is the solar image of Apollo, as the sun and gold in the UnderWorld, in the center. While we may reasonably interpret these figures as being literally the metals, at a deeper level of understanding we find that they embody the spiritual forces of the Seven Luminaries that manifest energetically through the physical metals.

By conscious sacromagical work with the spiritual forces of the UnderWorld and OverWorld, we may transform the elements and metals within our body and blood. The methods of the Sphere of Art enable such a transformation. This is the true alchemy from within, which in turn enables transformation of the outer world of nature.

(With thanks to Harry Vincent who identified the relationship between the historic illustration and the Sphere of Art methods described in this book.)

R. J. Stewart, California 2008

Table One

Sequence of publications and themes in chronological order of writing, leading to the development of The Sphere of Art.

Sacromagical Arts

1. The Underworld Initiation
2. Living Magical Arts
3. Advanced Magical Arts
4. Music and the Elemental Psyche
5. Music Power Harmony
6. The Miracle Tree
7. The Spirit Cord
8. The Sphere of Art

UnderWorld and Earth based spirituality

1. The UnderWorld Initiation
2. Earth Light
3. The Dreampower Tarot
4. Power Within the Land
5. The Well of Light

From Bardic Tradition

1. The Prophetic Vision of Merlin
2. The Mystic Life of Merlin
3. The Merlin Tarot
4. The Way of Merlin

Illustrations

Figure One: The Complete Tree of Life

From *The UnderWorld Initiation*, 1985, and subsequently in other titles.

Figure Two: The Body and the Seven Directions

From *Power Within the Land*, 1991.

Figure Three: The Directions within the Sphere

From *Advanced Magical Arts*, 1988

Figure Four: The Three Worlds and Three Wheels
(numbers refer to trump sequence in The Merlin Tarot)

From *Advanced Magical Arts*, 1988

Figure Five: The Dragon Arch and Gate Opening Symbol

Includes The Gate Opening Symbol from *The Merlin Tarot*, 1987; *Advanced Magical Arts*, 1988; *Power Within the Land*, 1992, and other publications. This key image has been used in publication and in Inner Temple Traditions Inner Convocation work from 1987 to the present day.

All titles have later editions in the USA and UK.
All figures copyright © R. J. Stewart

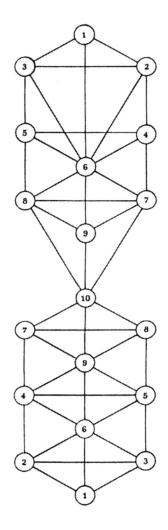

Figure 1
The complete Tree of Life

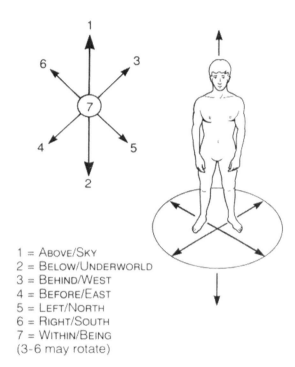

1 = Above/Sky
2 = Below/Underworld
3 = Behind/West
4 = Before/East
5 = Left/North
6 = Right/South
7 = Within/Being
(3-6 may rotate)

Figure 2
The Body and the Seven Directions

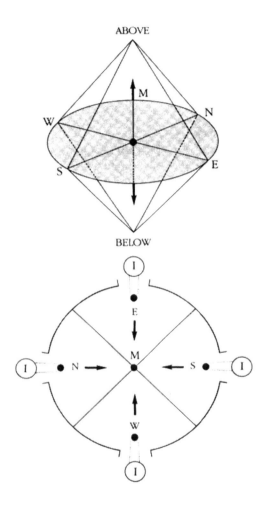

Figure 3
The Directions within the Sphere

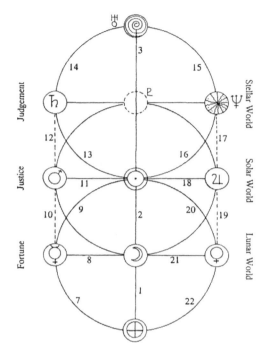

Wheel Three: The Stellar World, centred upon the Unknown Void

  ⬤ *Primum Mobile / seed and first utterance of Being*
  ○ *The Abyss or Void*
  ⊙ *Transpersonal consciousness (reflects or utters lower*
     consciousness)
  ♄ *Universal Understanding*
  Ψ *Universal Wisdom*

Figure 4
The Three Worlds and Three Wheels
(numbers refer to trump sequence in The Merlin Tarot)

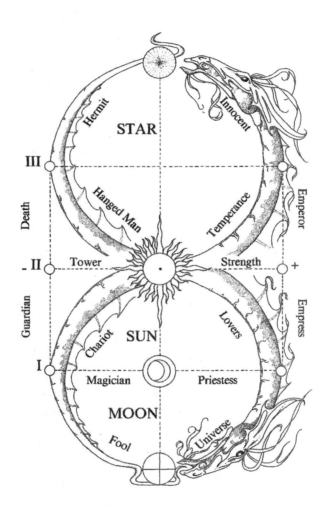

Figure 5
The Dragon Arch and Gate Opening Symbol

Figure Five

This image of the Dragons can be rendered as a glyph or simple symbol, and in this shape (as shown below) it appears in *Advanced Magical Arts* (1988) and *Power Within the Land* (1992) as The Gate Opening Symbol, and has been used in the Inner Temple/Inner Convocation sacromagical techniques from the early 1980's to the present day.

The theme of the Red and White Dragons, Evolutionary and Involutionary Streams, and Rivers of Blood and Tears has been published extensively in my books, most recently The Well of Light (2006). These concepts are shown by both the Dragon illustration and its simple glyph. In our present context we touch briefly upon some of the hidden possibilities, which will be developed at length in Volume Two. The reader should study the earlier texts and methods for essential background. The first presentation of this theme was in early 1980's in The Merlin Tarot texts, where the Tree of Life is shown as the Dragons, or the Evolutionary and Involutionary Streams. By the later 1980's, the use of a simple glyph had been developed, taught in workshops, and published. This glyph is more than a symbolic reduction of the Tree of Life (as that is basic geometry), for with initiated understanding within the Sphere of Art, it acts as a key to inner contact. In my earlier UnderWorld publications, the glyph, representing the power of the Dragons in the UnderWorld, was associated with an order of transhuman mentors (see Power Within the Land): illustrations of the glyph were published with associated guided visions, as an initial level of work. The complete Tree of Life is present in both UnderWorld and OverWorld, as in our Figure One. The glyph and the dragons are both ways of revealing a fusion of spiritual forces, and a higher octave of this fusion is generated within the Sphere of Art. In our Volume Two we will explore how to apply this further.

Bibliography and Notes

Some references are from internet sources and are given as URLs where you will find comprehensive bibliographies. Traditionally books are cited by their first published edition; some of the titles listed here are recent editions, as these are most readily available. If the note is edition specific, only that edition is cited.

Use of Wikipedia.org: Wikipedia is not a consistently reliable reference source, due to the process of submission and assembly, so the researcher must always check references carefully. Wikipedia references listed below have all been verified, and are listed either because they are unique and well-researched (as in the case of the Luis Rota material) or because they offer rapid access to substantial reference lists for further reading.

[1] Steiner, Rudolph, *Pyschoanalysis and Spiritual Pyschology* New edition. New York,1990. ISBN-10: 0880103515 ISBN-13: 978-0880103510. Earlier editions of these lectures are available. Also ed. Stewart, R.J. *Psychology and the Spiritual Traditions*, Shaftesbury, 1990.

[2] Fulcanelli: *La Mystere des Cathedrals* (trans) London 1971,/ Albuquerque NM 1991, ISBN 0914732145. The identity of Fulcanelli as Schwaller de Lubicz has been examined by French author Genevieve Dubois in *Fulcanelli and the Alchemical Revival* (trans) Rochester, VT, 2006. This well-researched book includes information on pivotal figures in the French alchemical revival. Other titles from Ms Dubois are recommended for further reading.

[3] http://www.wikirota.org/. The British author of this site, Mike Watson, also provided me with helpful information on the New Power

Rotor Trust, which was established by A R Heaver and others prior to the Second World War, as follows: "The NPR Trust existed to finance (the German physicist) Karl Schappeller to produce a demonstration model of his device for powering ships; a ships motor that needed no fuel...His machine mechanized a discovery he made of a form-building energy which exists in nature and is the driver of the life process (exactly what the alchemists were after) the vital force in fact, this energy takes disorder and reorders it, as in seed of a plant where manure is finally converted into a rose. The German secret societies called this energy "Vril" after the hypothetical force in Bulwer Lytton's 19th century novel. ...Schappeller was in the line of the alchemists like Schwaller de Lubicz and so on who knew that the secret fire was none other than the vital force... trying at least in the metallic process to use it to grow the metallic seed, except that Schappeller proposed to grow pure energy not matter...The NPR Trust fizzled out at the beginning of the war and Schappeller died in 1947."

[4] Inner Temple Traditions/Inner Convocation comprises a network of groups and classes, started in 1988 and continuing to the present day. For further information go to www.rjstewart.org.

[5] Spence, L. 1926 /2003, *The History of Atlantis*, Mineola, NY: Dover Publications. ISBN 0-486-42710-2. This study of Atlantis is especially relevant to the western esoteric tradition, as Spence was an initiate. Substantial Atlantis references are cited at http://en.wikipedia.org/wiki/Atlantis.

[6] Kingsley, P.: *Ancient Philosophy, Mystery, and Magic: Empedocles and Pythagorean Tradition*. Oxford,1997 ISBN-13: 9780198150817 ISBN: 0198150814. Other resources: http://en.wikipedia.org/wiki/Empedocles.

[7] A comprehensive article, including substantial reference sources is can be found at: http://en.wikipedia.org/wiki/Rosicrucian.

[8] Stewart R.J. *The UnderWorld Initiation, The Crossroads and the Rivers of Tears and Blood Revisited*. First published in *The Cauldron*, November 2005, UK. Also published in [9] and at http://www.rjstewart.org/tears-blood.html.

[9] Stewart, R.J. *The Spirit Cord* 2006 ISBN 978-0-9791402-0-4.

[10] Stewart, R.J. *The Myth of King Bladud*, Bath City 1980, The Waters of the Gap, Bath City 1981 and subsequent editions ISBN 1-85398-012-9. Levis, H. C, *The British King Who Tried to Fly*. Bath, 1919 reprinted 1973.

[11] A description and substantial reference sources for the legend of Prometheus can be found at http://en.wikipedia.org/wiki/Prometheus.

[12] Heaver, A. R. : Autobiographical essay, written circa 1965.

[13] See Table 1. *Living Magical Arts* , *Advanced Magical Arts*: Stewart,R J., Shaftesbury, UK 1985/1988 and 2006/2007 (revised editions) See also: Gray, W.G. *Magical Ritual Methods*, Teddington, Glos, UK, 1969. Knight, G. various titles. A list of books by Gareth Knight can be found at: http://www.angelfire.com/az/garethknight/books.html.

[14] Fortune, D. *The Mystical Qabalah*: Wellingborough1987, ISBN 0-85030-335-4, *The Cosmic Doctrine*, various editions. New edition published 2000, ISBN-13: 9781578631605 ISBN: 1578631602.

[15] See Table 1: *Earth Light, Power Within the Land, The Well of Light*. Also *Robert Kirk Walker Between Worlds: The Secret Commonwealth of Elves Fauns and Fairies 1692*. Ed. Stewart R.J. Shaftesbury 1990, new edition Roanoke, VA, 2007 ISBN: 9780979140242.

[16] Baudrillard, J. *Simulacra and Simulation*, (trans) 1995, ISBN-13: 9780472065219 ISBN: 0472065211.

[17] Townley, K. *Meditations on The Cube of Space*, 2000. ISBN-13: 9781931122092 ISBN: 1931122091.

[18] Stewart, R.J. *The Miracle Tree,* New Jersey, 2002 ISBN.

[19] Stewart R.J. Merlin, the Prophetic Vision and Mystic Life, Harmondsworth, 1986. ISBN-13: 9780140193725, ISBN: 0140193723. Knight, G, The Secret Tradition in Arthurian Legend, Wellingborough, 1983. ISBN-13: 9780850302936 ISBN: 0850302935.

[20] The American Heritage® Science Dictionary. See *Quantum Mechanics*.

[21] From The Internet Encyclopedia of Philosophy, *http://www.iep.utm. edu/h/husserl.htm*

[22] Stewart, R. J. *The Merlin Tarot*, Wellingborough, 1982 and many later editions.

[23] The Inner Temple CD series, in which the visualizations are recorded with original music, can be ordered from www.rjstewart.net.

Printed in the United States
129482LV00001B/130-177/P

9 780979 140266